The Masterpiece

The Life God Plans for You!

The Masterpiece

The Life God Plans for You!

Dr. Will Thomas

The Masterpiece is a revised and abridged version of a previously published work—*God Is At Work and the Difference It Makes (2023).*

All Bible quotations are from the New International Version unless otherwise noted. *New International Version,* Zondervan Publishing House, 2011.

To my three children in whom God continues to weave his masterpiece—Anthony, a devoted father and caring son; Angella, a godly woman with a will of steel and a heart of gold; and Adam, a man over-flowing with creativity and compassion. From a proud and grateful father.

Table of Contents

Epigraph

"For we are God's masterpiece. He has created us anew in Christ Jesus, so we can do the good things he planned for us long ago."

Ephesians 2:10 NLT

"Now faith is confidence in what we hope for and assurance about what we do not see."

Hebrews 11:1 NIV

"So we're not giving up. How could we! Even though on the outside it often looks like things are falling apart on us, on the inside, where God is making new life, not a day goes by without his unfolding grace. These hard times are small potatoes compared to the coming good times, the lavish celebration prepared for us. There's far more here than meets the eye. The things we see now are here today, gone tomorrow. But the things we can't see now will last forever."

2 Corinthians 4:16-18 MSG

Preface

Your life is a masterpiece! It may not feel like it, and, at times, it certainly may not look like it. Nonetheless, your life is a masterpiece the Lord is weaving one thread at a time. He weaves with an end in mind, even when we can't see it! How can life be a masterpiece but look like something completely different all at the same time? Because—life, yours and mine, is like a tapestry.

We have all seen some form of tapestry. Small ones might be framed and hung on the wall. Larger tapestries might come in the form of a fine carpet that graces the floor. Whatever the form, a tapestry is fabric art fashioned from various colors of thread that come together to form amazing patterns. Some can be realistic portraits of people or places, others awe-inspiring splashes of colors. Needlepoint, in some cases, might be considered a simple form of tapestry; a Persian rug a giant version.

For centuries, artists painstakingly fashioned tapestries by hand. A simple rug might take weeks, months, maybe even years to complete. In our age of computer-driven machines, factories can churn out a complicated product in mere minutes. And repeat it over and over again. Some tapestries are nothing short of spectacular, all done with fabric and thread. Delicate details and intricate patterns of colors are all made, whether by a computer or the hands of an artist, according to the plans of the designer.

Tapestries don't happen by accident. Nor does life! Like a tapestry, our Maker quietly, sometimes slowly, fashions all that we are into the masterpiece he envisions. In the middle of the process, we might not be able to figure out the picture that is coming together but rest assured the Artist knows. The Artist has a plan. Every thread and color change leads toward the intended goal. Life is like a tapestry!

However, here is our problem, a tapestry has two sides. The finished side reveals the mind of the maker, the picture the artist had in mind all along. But the other side, the underside, is another story. Even when completed, the backside of the tapestry makes little sense. It resembles a jumble of knots, loose threads, and chaotic colors. Even a studied eye has trouble detecting a pattern or purpose. If you watch an artist at work, but saw only the backside, you might think, "What a mess!" "Surely the weaver has made a mistake!" Rest assured, even in the midst of that mess, the artist has a plan. The artist weaves with the other side, the finished side, in mind.

Life is like a tapestry, and we live it on the backside!

We all do. Life, the way we live it, can be full of knots, loose ends, and a chaos of colors that seem to make no sense at all. We might conclude that all of this is headed nowhere. We can't detect a pattern or purpose. We can't imagine a finished product with any value. If we conclude by looking at the backside view, we would be wrong. Very wrong!

From the backside, life can seem meaningless, even hopeless. Nothing beautiful will ever come from this mess! That's a fair conclusion when all you know is the backside. But what if I could give you a glimpse, a sneak peek, at the other side? What if, all of a sudden, you know how it all fits together? What if the Maker allows you to see the masterpiece he had in mind? Would that make a difference? You bet it would! That's Ephesians!

Two Scriptural Foundations

Two verses of scripture drive this study. We will be drawn to the first often in the pages that follow. Ephesians 2:10 declares, "For we are God's handiwork, created in Christ Jesus to do good works, which God prepared in advance for us to do." That word "handiwork" could be rendered "masterpiece," as in the New Living Translation. The word describes something carefully fashioned with a purpose and design in mind. That's your life as God intends it—a masterpiece!

The second passage to keep in mind comes from Hebrews 11. The Hebrew writer describes faith as *"confidence in what we hope for and assurance about what we do not see"* (11:1). Faith rests on two absolute bedrock foundations. First, there is more to life than right now. A better and brighter future lies ahead. The best is yet to come—because of the promises and faithfulness of God. A person of faith lives life knowing that today, right now, is not all there is!

Second, faith knows that there is more to life than the obvious. Reality is more than flesh and blood, sticks and stones, or gold and silver. *"The conviction of things not seen!"* A spiritual world really exists. That spiritual world gives meaning and depth to life. Without an awareness of the invisible, life is shallow and pointless, a mere vapor that quickly evaporates into nothing. The underside of the tapestry is not the whole story. That's the perspective of 2 Corinthians 4:18, "*So we fix our eyes not on what is seen, but on what is unseen, since what is seen is temporary, but what is unseen is eternal.*"

What follows is not a detailed study of Ephesians. It is not intended to be. I term it a "devotional commentary." Our task is to listen to Paul, not argue with him or attempt to dissect his every word and phrase. We will look at enough of the details, but our focus is the big picture. We want to think about Paul's thoughts after him to better understand "the mystery of Christ" (Eph 3:4). That's what the apostle promised those who read his letter.

Ephesians is one of the rare jewels of the Bible. It is a treasure trove of riches, ready and waiting to be explored. Three golden threads weave their way through every chapter. Miss them and you will miss much that God has in store for you. First, Ephesians assumes the sovereignty of God. He is real. He is present. And He is at work in our world and our lives. Paul's Lord was God of the present, not just the past. Next, Ephesians is a book of grace. The God who made us is the God who loves us and wants to bless us. He proved that in Christ and continues to demonstrate it every day, in ways seen and unseen. Finally, Ephesians is a call to servanthood. God works through and in his people. He pours his grace into our hearts and expects his grace to flow through us into the lives of those around us.

When these three come together—grace, servanthood, and the sovereignty of God—the result is a masterpiece. Before our very eyes, we will experience and those around us will see—God at work!

I invite you to join me on a journey to the intersection of these three streams—grace, servanthood, and the sovereignty of God. Our tour guide for the trip will be Paul of Tarsus; our map, his ancient letter known to us as Ephesians. As for me, I am a fellow traveler.

Chapter One: Describing

Rainbows to the Blind

Paul, an apostle of Christ Jesus by the will of God, To God's holy people in Ephesus, the faithful in Christ Jesus: Grace and peace to you from God our Father and the Lord Jesus Christ. Praise be to the God and Father of our Lord Jesus Christ, who has blessed us in the heavenly realms with every spiritual blessing in Christ. For he chose us in him before the creation of the world to be holy and blameless in his sight. In love he predestined us for adoption to sonship through Jesus Christ, in accordance with his pleasure and will— to the praise of his glorious grace, which he has freely given us in the One he loves. In him we have redemption through his blood, the forgiveness of sins, in accordance with the riches of God's grace that he lavished on us. With all wisdom and understanding, he made known to us the mystery of his will according to his good pleasure, which he purposed in Christ, to be put into effect when the times reach their fulfillment—to bring unity to all things in heaven and on earth under Christ. In him we were also chosen, having been predestined according to the plan of him who works out everything in conformity with the purpose of his will, in order that

Ephesians 1:1-14

Ephesians is the story of the two sides of the masterpiece God is weaving. The Apostle Paul writes to people living on the underside. They can only see the work in progress, not the finished product. Paul writes to offer them a glimpse of the other side. He tells them what the Weaver has in mind and challenges them to live on the underside like they know the grand plan of their Maker. He wants to let them in on God's eternal secret.

The Underside of Life

Those early Christians in Ephesus to whom this portion of scripture was first penned lived on the underside. Ephesus was a large city for the day, the most prominent in the region. Corrupt politicians and the Roman army made sure Ephesus never forgot who controlled their lives. Several pagan temples crowned the city's landscape. Each featured its own version of superstition and decadence. Some majored in drunkenness, others in lust and sexual depravity. Much of the population lived in mortal fear of powerful evil spirits that they believed ruled their lives and had to be kept at bay through sacrifices and magic rituals.

That's what Paul walked into when he first came to Ephesus with the message of Jesus five or six years before he penned the letter to these young Christians. No one present would ever forget the series of strange events that accompanied the founding of that fledgling church (Acts 19). No sooner had Paul arrived than he met a group of men who claimed to be followers of Christ, yet something wasn't quite right. When Paul asked if they had received the Holy Spirit when they first believed, they claimed to not even know what he was talking about. They knew about Jesus but not about any ongoing ministry of the Holy Spirit. They knew some of the Christian message but not the full story. Paul corrected that problem.

A bit later, the sons of a prominent Jewish rabbi attempted to cast out a demon and were sent running for their lives when the demon countered, "Who are you? We know Jesus and we know Paul. We don't know you." Paul and his gospel were even famous in "hell."

Soon revival broke out as the gospel of Jesus spread from home to home. People began to throw off their superstitions and fear of the magical spirits that were supposed to rule their lives. People publicly burned their magic books and spirit idols. The revival so impacted the city that the silversmiths who made a nice living selling special idols and good luck charms to ward off the evil spirits complained that the new Christian sect was killing their business. A riot was erupted, and only at the last minute was peace restored. When Paul eventually left Ephesus after two or three years for other mission fields, a young, growing, vibrant congregation of believers remained, but it was a church surrounded by a hostile culture.

A few years later, while traveling to Jerusalem to deliver a special offering for the famine-stricken believers in Judea, Paul stopped nearby for a brief visit with the elders of the Ephesian church (Acts 20). He commended them for their faithfulness and warned of false teachers who would arise from within. Sometime after Paul penned this letter of Ephesians, he wrote to a young protégé, Timothy, with advice for his ministry with the church at Ephesus. He called for an emphasis on quality leaders, devotion to the study of scripture, and living out faith in Christ in the practical relationships of life. A generation later, John in the book of Revelation would declare Jesus' last word to the Ephesian church (Revelation 2:1-7). He would commend them for their zeal for correct doctrine and warned them about losing their first love. An allegiance to truth without love always does more harm than good.

As Paul pens this letter to the Ephesians, Paul sits under house arrest in faraway Rome. He had been arrested in Jerusalem, mostly for protective custody, and whisked away to Caesarea to foil a would-be assassination attempt by Jewish conspirators. When his case became ensnared in Judean political corruption, Paul appealed his case to Caesar. So off to Caesar he went, at Rome's expense! Once in the capital, the authorities allowed him to rent his own accommodations and receive visitors, all the while under guard (Acts 21-28).

Sometime during his house arrest, a runaway slave from Colossae finds his way to Paul. They might have met previously during Paul's year of ministry in the area. At any rate, Paul introduces Onesimus to Christ and persuades him he needs to make things right with his former master, Philemon, also a Christian. Paul sends Onesimus back with an accompanying letter to Philemon. Tychius, a Christian brother and co-worker of Paul, joins Onesimus on the journey back to his master. Paul uses the occasion of Tychicus' trip to send a letter to the Christians in Colossae and a second similar letter to the believers in Ephesus and perhaps the surrounding area.

The Key That Unlocks Ephesians

Ephesians divides into two big sections. Chapters 1-3 present an awe-inspiring outline of God's grand plan, the Master Weaver's pattern. These three chapters offer glimpses of the frontside of the tapestry of life. Chapters 4-6 provide instructions for those who are still living on the backside. In a sense, it says, "Now that you have seen what the Weaver is up to, what are you going to do about it." Once you know what's on the other side, your life on this side can never be the same. You may still live on the backside with all the knots, loose ends, and chaos of colors, but you can now live as topside people.

Ephesus 3:13 may be the key that unlocks the entire letter. "*I ask you, therefore, not to be discouraged because of my sufferings for you, which are your glory.*" Paul knows his Christian friends have heard about his plight. They are worried about him. He wants to encourage them. Everything he writes has one purpose—to convince his friends that God has everything under control. Regardless of what it might look like, God was at work. The Heavenly Father had big plans for them. He always had. Nothing had changed. God was putting together a masterpiece that he would one day reveal. If only they could see it now.

Explaining a Rainbow to a Blind Man

Herein the problem lies—how do you explain the frontside of the tapestry to someone who only knows the backside? Perhaps it would be like describing the colors of a rainbow or the golden hues of a sunset to a man born blind. Believe me, I have tried. I have a friend whom I first met when I worked with university students years ago. Technically, Ken probably had sight at birth. But when he was born very premature, the doctors put him in an incubator with oxygen and warming lights. They hadn't yet learned to protect the eyes of the little preemie. Ken, like many premature babies of that era, lost his sight as a result of the process that saved his life.

Ken went to a school for the blind, learned Braille, graduated high school, and eventually ended up at the university where I met him. We had some interesting conversations. Sometimes in his more pensive moments, he would ask me about things in the sighted world. We would talk about colors. Think about it. He had never seen the world you and I live in. He could hear it and feel it and smell it. But he had never *seen* it. He would listen to his friends talk about the Oklahoma football team's red uniforms. Ken had never seen black or white, or green or blue, much less crimson and cream. He knew the words but not the reality.

I would ask him what went through his head when he heard such words. He explained that he associated colors with touch. Some colors made him think of rough or smooth, hot or cold. He had nothing else with which he could associate the colors we take for granted. He had no idea what we experience when we see the sunset over the water or the rainbow appear against an azure sky.

That's the challenge of Ephesians. How do you explain the Weaver's plan to those who have only seen knots and loose ends?

Your Life Is Not an Accident

Ephesians begins with the greeting typical to ancient letters. Paul identifies himself and acknowledges his intended readers. Any young Greek or Roman student would have learned the protocols of letter writing in the early years of school. Times and communication styles may have changed, but the same principles apply. Most correspondences include an address, a greeting, the information, and a closing salutation. We may scramble the order a bit, but it's all still there, in one form or another.

Note the emphasis on the will of God. Paul is absolutely convinced that his life and ministry are no accidents. God was at work. Likewise, he knows that the believers who will read his words are God's people. The Almighty works in their lives, seen or unseen. That's foundational to everything that follows.

Ephesians 1:3-14 is actually one long sentence in the original language. It is as if the words bubbled over as Paul tries to describe the indescribable. The reality of the frontside of the tapestry defied every attempt to put it into words.

"Praise be the God and Father of our Lord Jesus Christ, who has blessed us ...." The first words matter. Anyone who gets a glimpse of the other side and begins to understand the pattern the Maker is weaving, can have only one reaction—Praise God! All glory to him! God is good—all the time! What he is doing makes the knots and loose ends we live with worth it. They no longer matter because we know he is planning a masterpiece!

This whole first sentence, in fact, all of the first three chapters of Ephesians, form a doxology or a declaration of praise to God. Time after time, Paul's words overflow in worship. To the praise of his glorious grace...for the praise of his glory...to the praise of his glory. To know what God is making of us is to marvel at his glorious grace.

When Paul says, "Praise be God...who has blessed us in the heavenly realms with every spiritual blessing in Christ," think about the other side of the weaving. The blessings are there. We may not see them from the underside. But if we could see the other side, our doubts would vanish. We are blessed!

Everything Is Under Control

Several ideas stand out in this very complex sentence. First, did you catch the emphasis on the Triune Godhead—God the Father, Jesus Christ the Savior, and the promised Holy Spirit? Remember, we are describing a rainbow to a blind man. So don't get overly concerned about being able to connect all the dots. We can't expect to understand everything about the character and nature of God. If we did, we would be God or at least his equal. We are not! We are finite, limited human beings. Even in eternity, God will be God, and we won't.

Note the focus on God's plan. What is happening in our lives, on this side of life, is no accident. He chose us before the foundations of the world. He predestined us for adoption. He is moving us toward holiness. He has a finished product in mind. Ultimately everything will come together. When all is said and done, all that has happened and has yet to happen will make sense in light of Jesus Christ. Don't give up too soon. Give the Weaver time to work his wonders.

We can easily overthink this language of God's choosing and predestining. All it is saying is that God's got this. Everything is under control, even though it might not look like it at any given moment. Remember, we only see the underside of the weaving. What might look like chaos from where we stand is really his plan coming together. When the last thread is woven into the plan, we will only be able to say, "Wow. Blessed be God!"

Our God Has a Plan

A couple of things about God's plan. It is about him, Christ Jesus. Being in him is a place of security and peace. He is the ultimate safe space. The faith that rests on things unseen and still hoped for finds its fulfillment in Jesus. We live with our eyes fixed on him (Hebrews 12:2). Secondly, God plans to make something of us. This life is a preparation for the next. Everything that has happened in your life has served to make you fit for eternity, more and more like Jesus every day. You can fight his plan and suffer the consequences. You will encounter more and more knots and loose ends as life unfolds. Or you can let him weave the masterpiece he intends.

Jesus is the only one that can make sense of it all. He explains God. Jesus himself said that all of the Old Testament was about him. He didn't mean that every story and person was really Jesus in disguise. Not at all. The whole Bible IS about Jesus. The whole

Bible *is* about Jesus in the sense that the whole thing leads to him. It all points to him. Without him, it makes no sense. With him, it will ultimately all come together. He fulfills it!

You can't understand this long sentence that launches Ephesians without being overwhelmed with God's love. Note the language Paul uses. "In love, he predestined us for adoption…to the praise of his glorious grace…we have redemption…in accordance with the riches of God's grace that he lavished on us."

Praise God! He has a plan. It focuses on Jesus. When it all comes together, Jesus will be the center of it all. From beginning to end, his design flows from love, more love than we can fathom. We may live on the underside of the tapestry, but we are not alone. Did you catch that last part of the sentence? *"And you also were included in Christ when you heard the message of truth, the gospel of your salvation. When you believed, you were marked in him with a seal, the promised Holy Spirit, who is a deposit guaranteeing our inheritance until the redemption of those who are God's possession…"* Paul will come back to this again and again. Remember his encounter with the uninformed disciples when he first came to Ephesus. "Did you receive the Holy Spirit when you first believed?" They may not be the only ones who need to be asked that question. The fact is— God has not left us to our own devices. When we came to Christ, he entered us through the Holy Spirit. He is working from the inside out to guide, strengthen, and protect us. That's our guarantee that the best is yet to come. The presence of the Holy Spirit is the down payment" (Eph 1:13-14).

God's calling and predestining don't require us to believe that God directly causes everything that happens—including bad things and evil itself. Some come to that conclusion because they overthink and over define these terms. Some of us arrogantly act as if we couldn't possibly accept God's plan unless he first explains it to us in detail. Sometimes it sounds as if we were suggesting that God is only free to be God after we understand and approve. We forget that from our side of the tapestry, God's plan will always have loose ends and unanswered questions. Someday we will see the other side. Then all will be clear. For now, we must allow God to be God without limiting him to our abilities to understand.

God's Grand Plan—You Are Included

Here's the key lessons Paul wants us to know about the master's grand plan, lessons that should affect how we live on this side of the tapestry:

First, God has a plan. We are not an accident. Nothing has been left to chance. The Weaver is at work. He has it all under control. Even if we can't see it from the underside, each loose end, tangled thread, and jumbled knot has a place in the pattern he is weaving. It may sometimes look like chaos from the underside, but from above, it's a different story.

This is not a new plan. The Creator of heaven and earth didn't decide at the last minute that he had to do something. I have no idea what all of this means in human terms, but the message is clear. The plan is well thought out. He set it in motion long before we entered the picture.

Next, God is weaving a blessing, not a curse. It will work together for something good, whether or not it seems like it at the moment. We can endure what's happening on the underside because we know it is all part of the spiritual blessings God is fashioning on the other side, in heavenly places. His plan flows from love. It includes redemption, forgiveness, and so much more. The only description that even comes close to sufficient—it is according to "the riches of his grace." God even weaves with broken threads!

Also, the end product of God's plan is that we be holy (devoted to Him, kept pure for his use). This matters because he has reserved a place for us in his family. That's how much he loves us. He intends to adopt us. We will be sons and daughters, not slaves. That's what our God is working on for us. This has been his plan all along. When we get a glimpse of the other side, the final product, the only thing we can do is praise his amazing grace.

If we could see the other side, the plan he is working on, we would begin to understand what the gospel has been telling us from the very beginning. Christ Jesus made it all possible through the cross. His sacrifice purchased our redemption, our freedom from sin. He set us free, forgave us our sins, and ushered us into a totally new relationship with the God who made us. We may not understand how it all fits together, but one day we will. It is as if Paul were saying to us, "If you only could see it now, you would understand." God loves you more than you can possibly imagine. Someday it will all be clear.

Christ is what holds it all together. He is the key to God's plan for you. Our future is in his hands. Everything we will be, everything God has in store for us in the future, will come from what Christ has made possible for us. This is the plan. This is what he is weaving on the other side. When we finally see it, we will understand and praise him for it. It is good to start practicing our gratitude now—even in advance. He has it all under control. That is our confidence, our faith, and steadfast hope.

We all stepped into this grand plan the day we put our faith in him. Somebody explained the message of Jesus to us. We heard and believed. We were saved. Our destiny was sealed. The Holy Spirit marked us and began a work in us that will continue until the day God completes his masterpiece. On that day, we will finally move from the underside. Then and only then will we be able to look down at what the Lord has been weaving day in and day out in our lives. What we don't understand now, we will understand then. All the loose ends, tangled knots, and confusing colors will become an amazing portrait of God's wisdom and grace.

Paul knows that his words don't do the reality of God's plan justice. There is much that defies explanation. If only we could see it for ourselves! Only God can make that happen. Oh, that he would. That's what Paul has been praying for on behalf of his Ephesians friends. I suspect he would pray the same for us.

✝

Chapter Two: With Eyes Wide Open

For this reason, ever since I heard about your faith in the Lord Jesus and your love for all God's people, I have not stopped giving thanks for you, remembering you in my prayers. I keep asking that the God of our Lord Jesus Christ, the glorious Father, may give you the Spirit of wisdom and revelation, so that you may know him better. I pray that the eyes of your heart may be enlightened in order that you may know the hope to which he has called you, the riches of his glorious inheritance in his holy people, and his incomparably great power for us who believe. That power is the same as the mighty strength he exerted when he raised Christ from the dead and seated him at his right hand in the heavenly realms, far above all rule and authority, power and dominion, and every name that is invoked, not only in the present age but also in the one to come. And God placed all things under his feet and appointed him to be head over everything for the church, which is his body, the fullness of him who fills everything in every way.

Ephesians 1:15-23

Paul has tried to explain what God is doing in the spiritual world that his readers can't see and may have difficulty understanding. They live on the underside of the tapestry. God is at work on both sides, but the believer can only see the underside. But faith makes the difference. "Faith is the assurance of things hoped for and the conviction of things unseen" (Heb 11:1)

Paul prays for the Ephesian believers because he knows God is at work in their lives, whether they can see and understand it or not. He knows they believe this. He knows they have demonstrated this faith in their love for one another and the people of God in other places. He wants them to know that he constantly thinks about them and prays for them. What does he pray for? Primarily one item in particular—he prays for their eyes to open. He prays that the Lord will enable them to catch a glimpse of what God is doing in the unseen world and the future he is weaving for them.

Paul asks that God would do a work of the "spirit" in them. Here, the term quite likely refers to the Holy Spirit, God's special and personal presence. But Paul leaves the specifics largely undefined. He could mean "spirit" in a more "human" sense, namely, that part of our nature made for a relationship with God. Either way, he prays for a work that only God can do. He asks that God develop in them "wisdom." That's a clear understanding of God's work. He adds "revelation" to that. Picture unveiling a priceless work of art that has been kept hidden or taking a blindfold off a person so she can now see what's happening. How does this wisdom and revelation come? Only through a deeper knowledge and closer relationship with God himself!

We will never solve the dilemmas of life by staring harder at our problems. But amazingly, the closer we get to our God, the better we will see what he is doing in us and for us. Our doubts and problems grow small as our faith grows large. Only as we get closer to the source of our light will we be able to see ourselves and the world around us. As C. S. Lewis said of his faith in Christ, "I believe that the sun has risen: not only because I see it, but because by it I see everything else."[1]

Paul prays that the eyes of their hearts will be enlightened. Clearly, this is a figure of speech for our inner spiritual understanding. A person can have 20-20 vision but be blind to the real issues of reality. That spiritual reality—the work God is doing in the unseen—includes the hope of our calling (the future God is building through our lives), the riches of his inheritance in the saints (all that Christ accomplished for us on the cross), and the greatness of his power at work in us (the present reality of God at work). Imagine the change that would take place if we really understood what the Lord was making of us, his plans and promises for us, and the real power available to us through his Spirit at work in us.

Having the Eyes of Your Heart Enlightened

Pretend that you are part of a football team. Minutes before the big game, all the players gather in the locker room, ready to head out onto the field. The coach calls for everyone's attention. He has some final words. He goes over the game plan. He paints a picture of what winning would mean to the team and the school. He challenges everyone to give their all for the next sixty minutes. Why the rousing pep talk? Every coach and player knows that much of winning or losing depends on attitude, not just ability. More than that, what matters most is the team's capacity to work together. Almost any team that plays as a team can defeat an even better squad that doesn't have a common vision or a team spirit. That's not just true in sports. It's true for a church, too! If you understand that, you will understand Paul's prayer.

Seeing means more than just catching light rays on the retina of our eyes. When we speak of seeing, we often mean understanding. To say, "I see what you mean," doesn't just imply that we witnessed someone talking to us. It means we saw, listened, heard, and grasped what was meant. We have all experienced watching something without really paying attention. We were looking but not focusing. Whatever happened slipped by without our noticing it.

We do it with sound all of the time. We hear without really listening. We can tune out background noise or what we choose not to hear. Wives and husbands often refer to this as "selective hearing." Mothers can hear a baby's cry at night but not hear the train two blocks away. A husband can hear the unusual rattle in the truck motor but not hear his wife's question during a ballgame.

Seeing and hearing are very much matters of focus. That was Paul's point. All of us have the ability to look at life from different viewpoints. We most often talk about it in terms of attitude, motivation, values and priorities. I think Paul's concern that his friends learn to "see with the eyes of their hearts" grew from personal experience. Remember what Paul said in 2 Corinthians 5, *"So from now on we regard no one from a worldly point of view. Though we once regarded Christ in this way, we do so no longer. Therefore, if anyone is in Christ, he is a new creation; the old has gone, the new has come!"* (16-17). The phrase in Verse 16 for "a worldly point of view" is literally "according to the flesh."

This is an important biblical concept. Sometimes the term "flesh" means "flesh and blood." But sometimes, it carries another meaning. As with the phrase "eyes of your heart" in Paul's prayer, seeing with your "flesh" implies far more than just looking at things with 20/20 eyesight. The NIV translation tries to get at this idea with the words "worldly point of view." This is not just seeing; it is focusing in a particular way. It is tuning in on certain things and tuning out other things.

Now contrast the two phrases in these two different texts (Eph 1:18 and 2 Cor 5:16). In the one, Paul speaks of "seeing with the eyes of the heart." In the other, he refers to no longer having a "worldly point of view." These are mirror images of each other. They are speaking of exactly the same phenomena, only from two opposite angles. To fail to "see with the eyes of your heart" is to have a "worldly perspective." One is to focus on the spiritual, the eternal, the godly, the lasting, the things of faith, hope, and love. The other is to see only the material, the financial, the temporal, and the ungodly things that produce and flow from cynicism, despair, and indifference. A "worldly perspective" lacks "confidence in what we hope for and assurance about what we do not see" (Heb 11:1).

Both conditions, both ways of seeing, are contagious—personally and socially. If you begin to look at one area of life through eternal eyes—from a perspective of faith—soon you are looking at everything that way. Conversely, a person with a worldly perspective about one thing will eventually find it spilling over into other areas of life. A man who is materialistic and greedy (this is part of a worldly perspective) in his business dealings will sooner or later begin to be materialistic with his family. Eventually, he may even become a materialistic church leader. Both ways of seeing can be contagious from one person to another. Like an eye infection that quickly passes from one to another, either eyes of faith or worldly perspectives can pass through families, businesses, clubs, and even churches, through conversation and example. Worldly perspectives can be unbelievably destructive. Beginning to see with the eyes of the heart can be equally powerful in the opposite direction.

But maybe what is most significant is the fact that a "worldly perspective" can be changed. Paul claimed his changed. He became a new creation (2 Cor 5:17). But he also insisted that the same thing could happen to others. That is why he prayed for his friends from Ephesus that the "eyes of their hearts" would be enlightened. The blind could be made to see!

Paul believed that was what it meant to become a Christian—a person's focus changed. A person started looking at Jesus, life, and other people completely differently than before. The change was so profound that it could be likened to walking out of the darkness into light. As the beloved hymn "Amazing Grace" words it, "I once was blind, but now I see."

Seeing With Job's Eyes

Finally, before we turn to the next section of our map of Ephesians, let's take a step back in time and in the pages of the Bible. Let's take a deep dive into a classic tale of faith under fire like few before or since. In the Old Testament story of Job, we find an example of life on the underside and the difference a glimpse of the other side can make. Consider how the Old Testament story begins and ends:

> *"In the land of Uz there lived a man whose name was Job. This man was blameless and upright; he feared God and shunned evil. He had seven sons and three daughters, and he owned seven thousand sheep, three thousand camels, five hundred yoke of oxen and five hundred donkeys, and had a large number of servants. He was the greatest man among all the people of the East"* (Job 1:1-3).

> *"After Job had prayed for his friends, the Lord restored his fortunes and gave him twice as much as he had before. All his brothers and sisters and everyone who had known him before came and ate with him in his house. They comforted and consoled him over all the trouble the Lord had brought on him, and each one gave him a piece of silver and a gold ring.*

> *The Lord blessed the latter part of Job's life more than the former part. He had fourteen thousand sheep, six thousand camels, a thousand yoke of oxen and a thousand donkeys. And he also had seven sons and three daughters. The first daughter he named Jemimah, the second Keziah and the third Keren-Happuch. Nowhere in all the land were there found women as beautiful as Job's daughters, and their father granted them an inheritance along with their brothers.*

Between these two texts, scripture records the ups and downs of Job's life. All was well for Job until it wasn't! His life fell apart so badly that the only rational conclusion was that he was on God's hit list. But why? That was the big question.

Job begins the poetic books of the Bible. As such, Job contains countless metaphors, word pictures, striking visual images, and imaginative dialogue. But the value of Job lies in more than its structure and literary form. Its story is compelling because it is so like the stories everyone faces—only written much larger. Job is about *the question.* C. S. Lewis called it the toughest faith question of all. Philosophers have asked the question since the beginning of time. Theologians have searched and searched for a satisfying answer. Everyone has wrestled with the personal side of the problem of pain.

In Job, the Bible tackles that age-old question of why bad things happen to good people. It is a defense against the charge that either God is not good (he makes bad things happen unfairly) or he is not powerful (he can't stop bad things when they happen). Job's forty-two chapters divide into four main sections: (1) 1-3, a prologue explaining the background, occasion, and terrible suffering of Job; (2) 4-37, the human solutions proposed by four friends; (3) 38-42, God's answer and Job's response; (4) 42:10-17, an epilogue detailing the great return of Job's blessings.

Now for the story! Job was a prosperous Middle Eastern prince. He was a wealthy man. He had ten children, seven sons and three daughters, and countless servants. He was also a religious man. Job was a good man known in both heaven and earth for his righteousness.

The Unseen Side of the Story

Meanwhile another story is unfolding—in heaven. Somehow or another (the Bible offers no explanation or details), when the angels came before the Lord, the Accuser, likely understood as Satan, the fallen angel, was among them. The Lord engages the Accuser in conversation about—of all things—Job. The Lord points out the righteousness of Job. The Accuser lives up to his title. "Sure, he is," Satan counters. "Anyone would be good if you blessed him as much as you have Job. Take away all the riches and prosperity and see what Job does."

The Lord accepts the challenge and permits Satan to test Job. This is when disaster strikes. Job knows nothing of the drama in heaven. He only knows what happens to him on his side of eternity. First, he lost his flocks and herds and houses. One day he was wealthy beyond measure. The next day he was destitute. Then he lost his family. A windstorm blew down a family home, killing all of his children and many servants. One day Job had a family. The next day Mr. and Mrs. Job were alone. Eventually, he lost his health. His body was ravaged with terrible sores. When friends came to visit, they hardly recognized his disfigured body.

Job was shaken to his foundation. He grieved. He wept. He cried to God for an answer. Friends and family turned against him. At one point, he wished he could die or better yet had never been born. But while everyone around him gave up on Job, Job never gave up on God. Listen to what happened when Job learned of his children's death, "*At this, Job got up and tore his robe and shaved his head. Then he fell to the ground in worship and said: "Naked I came from my mother's womb, and naked I will depart. The LORD gave and the LORD has taken away; may the name of the LORD be praised." In all this, Job did not sin by charging God with wrongdoing*" (1:20-22).

The bulk of the book explores the possible explanations for Job's calamity. First, there is the answer of Job's wife. We do need to cut Mrs. Job some slack. She, too, lost everything. The only thing she kept that her husband lost was her health. But during Job's darkest hour, she told her suffering husband, "*Are you still holding on to your integrity? Curse God and die!*" (Job 2:9). Nothing like a little support from the better half!

Mrs. Job's response is not all that uncommon. Religion ought to make you healthy, wealthy, and wise—so the argument goes. If it doesn't, what's the point? Such a faith holds on only so long as it is convenient or profitable. That was Satan's theory. "Take away the blessing and the faith will disappear!" The advice is bad. Job's response was good. He told his wife, "*You are talking like a foolish woman. Shall we accept good from God, and not trouble?*" (2:10).

Next, Job's three friends show up, each with different angles on the same opinion. At three different times, they each contend with Job, arguing that he suffers because he is guilty of some terrible sin. Many people believe a similar notion, even if they don't word it like Job's friends. It's similar to a belief in Karma, the Hindu doctrine of cause and effect. Karma insists that bad things don't happen to good people. Bad things happen to bad people! Suffering comes from the consequences of bad acts in this or a past life. Do good and good things will follow.

Eliphaz, the first friend, argues, "*Consider now: Who, being innocent, has ever perished? Where were the upright ever destroyed?*" (Job 4:7-8). Bildad, the second friend, follows the same line of reasoning. "*Does God pervert justice? Does the Almighty pervert what is right? When your children sinned against him, he gave them over to the penalty of their sin*" (Job 8:3-4). Later he argues, "*Surely such is the dwelling of an evil man; such is the place of one who knows not God*" (Job 18:21). Zophar, the third friend, not only says Job must be guilty of some secret sin. In addition, *God has probably forgotten some of his sins* (11:6). Job not only deserves what he has gotten, Zophar insists, he probably deserves far worse.

Each time Job withstands the attack of his friends and insists that he has done nothing to deserve his situation. The friends grow more determined. Job is not only a sinner but also an arrogant, unrepentant one. Ultimately, Job's three friends offer little comfort and a great deal of condemnation. With friends like these, who needs enemies! Later, God clearly rejects the counsel of all three friends.

The next attempt at an explanation comes from Elihu, a young friend who simply sat and listened through much that transpired. But finally, Elihu breaks his silence. What he says carries a fair amount of truth. In fact, it is pretty close to the advice the Bible offers elsewhere. Elihu suggests that the suffering has a purpose. Maybe God is trying to teach Job something or perhaps even warn him of some sin yet uncommitted. *"He [God] may speak in their ears and terrify them with warnings, to turn man from wrongdoing and keep him from pride, to preserve his soul from the pit, his life from perishing by the sword" (Job 33:16-18).*

Elihu suggests that Job's stubbornness may be the root of the problem. It is not that Job had previously committed some sin. Instead, God sent the torment to reveal the sin of rebellion hidden deep in Job's heart. "*Oh, that Job might be tested to the utmost for answering like a wicked man! To his sin he adds rebellion; scornfully he claps his hands among us and multiplies his words against God*" (Job 34:36-37).

We can't argue with Elihu's reasoning. It is at least partly true. This was the gist of C. S. Lewis' conclusion in *The Problem of Pain*. Lewis' story was made famous in the much-acclaimed movie *Shadowlands* starring Anthony Hopkins. In the midst of great grief at the loss of his new wife, Lewis declares, "God whispers in our pleasures, but he shouts in our pain."[2] Sometimes suffering contains God's voice.

Hard times do make stronger people. Sometimes the refiner's fire has one purpose—to take away the impurities and make us better. But Elihu's counsel didn't offer much comfort to a grieving, broken man who had lost everything but his faith. One voice remains to be heard, the only voice that Job wants to hear. God alone holds the answer to his struggle. Job laments, *"I cry out to you, O God, but you do not answer; I stand up, but you merely look at me"* (Job 30:20).

Finally, Heaven Speaks

Finally, God breaks his silence and speaks from a storm. The entire book has been leading to this all along. When we turn the page to this section, we almost hold our breath. What will God say? What will *his* answer be? For four chapters, God speaks. And he doesn't provide a single answer! For the better part of 130 verses, God just asks questions. *"Who is this that darkens my counsel with words without knowledge? Brace yourself like a man; I will question you, and you shall answer me. "Where were you when I laid the earth's foundation? Tell me, if you understand. Who marked off its dimensions? Surely you know! Who stretched a measuring line across it? On what were its footings set, or who laid its cornerstone—while the morning stars sang together and all the angels shouted for joy"* (Job 38:2-7)?

One question after another! Not a single answer, just questions! But Job is satisfied! He has found the answer for which he yearned in a barrage of divine questions. He finally sees what had been invisible. Job's friends had foolishly offered hopeless help. All the time, another drama was playing out in heaven. Job couldn't see it. It remained invisible to his friends. Only when Job listens to God does he find peace and restoration. He learned that God had been faithfully weaving on the other side what Job nor his friends could see from their side.

The answer: Life sometimes hurts. It isn't always fair. But even then, God is at work. And that's what matters. We will never have all the answers, but God does. And that is enough. The old hymn says, "I may not know what tomorrow holds, but I know who holds tomorrow." The Shepherd's Psalm hints at the same answer, "*Even though I walk through the darkest valley, I will fear no evil, for you are with me; your rod and your staff, they comfort me*" (Ps 23:4).

Romans 8, in many ways a commentary on the experiences of Job and every other person who has struggled with the underside of life, puts it this way, "*And we know that in all things God works for the good of those who love him, who have been called according to his purpose. . . .*
What, then, shall we say in response to these things? If God is for us, who can be against us? He who did not spare his own Son, but gave him up for us all—how will he not also, along with him, graciously give us all things" (Romans 8:28, 31-32).

Remember, Job lived on the other side of the cross. We see and know things that he could never know about God's mercy and grace. Paul prayed that "the eyes of your hearts might be enlightened" so that his readers could see the invisible, to recognize the faithful hand of their God even when it seemed like they had been abandoned. Job's God, and ours, is at work—even when we don't see it!

Chapter Three: Before and After

As for you, you were dead in your transgressions and sins, in which you used to live when you followed the ways of this world and of the ruler of the kingdom of the air, the spirit who is now at work in those who are disobedient. All of us also lived among them at one time, gratifying the cravings of our flesh and following its desires and thoughts. Like the rest, we were by nature deserving of wrath. But because of his great love for us, God, who is rich in mercy, made us alive with Christ even when we were dead in transgressions—it is by grace you have been saved. And God raised us up with Christ and seated us with him in the heavenly realms in Christ Jesus, in order that in the coming ages he might show the incomparable riches of his grace, expressed in his kindness to us in Christ Jesus. For it is by grace you have been saved, through faith—and this is not from yourselves, it is the gift of God—not by works, so that no one can boast. For we are God's handiwork, created in Christ Jesus to do good works, which God prepared in advance for us to do. therefore, remember that formerly you who are Gentiles by birth and called "uncircumcised" by those who call themselves "the circumcision" (which is done in the body by human hands)— remember that at that time you were separate from Christ, excluded from citizenship in Israel and

Ephesians 2:1-22

We live on the underside of life. We see the problems and tragedies common to our world. Seldom do we see the big picture, what God is doing to make things right. In Ephesians 1, Paul paints with broad strokes. In Chapter 2, he turns his attention to the personal. He explains what God has done and is doing in the lives of each believer. He wants his readers to understand that it's not just the world that is broken; so are they! But God specializes in using broken things and broken people. He has just one requirement—that the broken people he redeems and uses to further his plan never forget whose plan and power it is.

Paul moves from anticipating the rich future God is making for us (the end of Chapter 1) to the poverty that once marked our lives. As long as we deceive ourselves about our past, we will never fully appreciate or understand our future in Christ. Paul paints a dark picture. But note the turnaround in Verse 4. "But because of his great love for us, God…" Truly, this is BC (before Christ) contrasted with AD (after God's intervention)!

In Chapter 1, Paul prayed that the Lord would open his readers' spiritual eyes. In the next chapter, he asks his readers to remove the barriers that prevent them from clearly seeing themselves. We all have five blind spots that keep us from appreciating what is truly a work of God in our lives. Like the prodigal son, we remain in the pig pen until we come to ourselves and begin to see who and where we are. Consider our common blind spots (Lk 15:13-19).

First, we deny how bad our situation really is. We tell ourselves this is only temporary. The pig pen is not really all that bad. We will never go home until we recognize that we are dead men walking—"dead in our trespasses and sins." Note the two terms—trespasses and sins—this covers it all. Trespasses are sins of commission, stepping over the line, and doing what we know is off-limits. The other is shortcomings, just not living up to our capabilities.

Secondly, we tell ourselves somebody else is at fault. On our own, we would never have gone that route. We aren't that bad after all. We really are good people—if you really get to know us. God knows otherwise. We were dead in trespasses and sins because we walked with the world. It wasn't just a momentary slip. The devil can't make us do anything without our willing participation. He lies to us. But his lies are only effective after we have believed the lies we tell ourselves.

Next, we convince ourselves that our sins are really the exception. That's not really us. We just made a momentary mistake. That, too, is a lie. Truth be told — we lived the way we wanted to live. We caved not to the devil's lures but to our own desires. The fact is something was wrong with us before we did wrong. The blame has to start with us. Until we accept that, we will forever remain mired in the pig pen.

The self-deception continues. We deserve mercy not punishment, we insist. Not true. We were headed for wrath. We are just as deserving of punishment by a holy God as anyone else in the world. We may tell ourselves that we are above average—not like those other people! If we think that way, we are the only ones who believe it. "We are by nature children of wrath, even as the rest."

Finally, the biggest blind spot is this: when after having been rescued from the destructive path we were on, we attempt to convince ourselves that we actually engineered our own escape. We pulled ourselves up by our own bootstraps and dug ourselves out of the pit. As long as we think that way, even a little bit, we will never see clearly what God is trying to make of us. *While we were yet sinners, Christ died for us!* (Rm 5:8).

That was the way we were before Christ. He changed us. We didn't deserve or earn his blessings. We received mercy. We know what we were and how God has dealt with us. We know why he saved us. And we know the reason he didn't save us—our own goodness. We have hope because of grace. That doesn't mean how we live now doesn't matter. Quite to the contrary! Because of what God has done in us, we want to live lives that honor and glorify him and bring benefit into the lives of others.

The Masterpiece God Makes

Paul is now ready to explain what happens when a person steps through the door into a new life in Christ. No doubt his readers had heard this before, as have we. But we forget. We can easily allow ourselves to think that maybe we had more to do with it than we did. We can begin to assume more credit than we deserve. That always leads to stealing the credit that belongs to somebody else. The next step takes us toward a sense of superiority. "If we were able to change so much *on our own,* then others can do the same." Anyone who doesn't quite measure up to us must not be as good as us. How could we ever view them as equals or brothers and sisters in Christ? Paul now moves to eliminate such thinking.

But! This is the keyword that begins the passage (vs. 4). It is a hinge word. Everything in the passage turns on this little word. *But* signals a contrast, a change of direction in the discussion. So far, Paul has insisted that there is more to life than what we see. God is at work. He has a masterplan and is weaving the pieces together. If we could only see it, we would understand what he is doing. That's all in Chapter 1.

In Chapter 2, he flashes back to what God has already done. He reminds his readers what they were before Christ entered their lives. It wasn't a pretty picture. Paul knows. This was his story too. But then it changed. But he/we are not what we used to be. Thank God! Once, he/we deserved wrath. But now we have received something totally different. The keyword is *received.* We are not responsible for what we have become. We are definitely responsible for what we were. But something changed, and we didn't do it. God did! It was a work of God.

Paul explains what God did. We were dead in our sins; then he made us alive. He raised us up. He seated us with him in heavenly realms. He reserved a seat for us at the heavenly banquet. On that grand day, we will all celebrate what he has done. He will unveil his work. All heaven and earth will see the masterpiece he has been putting together. And we are part of it. What a glorious day!

Note when God did this, we were the walking dead! We were dead in our transgressions. He didn't wait for us to clean ourselves up first. In Romans, Paul explains, *"You see, at just the right time, when we were still powerless, Christ died for the ungodly. Very rarely will anyone die for a righteous person, though for a good person someone might possibly dare to die. But God demonstrates his own love for us in this: While we were still sinners, Christ died for us"* (Rm 5:6-8).

Note why God did this. Because of his great love! Ultimately God does what he does because of his character, not ours. Our new relationship flows from who he is! He is rich in mercy. It is by grace that we have been saved not because of our merit or accomplishments. Two words need a clear definition—mercy and grace. They are clearly related, yet subtly distinct. Mercy is not getting what we deserve. In this case, forgiveness instead of wrath. Grace is receiving so much more than what we deserve. His love has abundantly overflowed with blessing upon blessing. In a sense, mercy reminds us of what we have been saved from; grace points to what we have been saved for. Both grace and mercy flow from the riches of his love. That's amazing—grace!

Note where this leaves us. We have nothing to boast about. We can never pat ourselves on the back and say, "Look at what I have done. I must be something special! God saved ME!" God is the special one. We are saved by his grace. We simply believed him and received what he freely offered. We are a product of his work, not our works. Anything good that comes out of me is because of what he has been weaving into my life and planning for me long before I ever realized he was at work. The only response I can give is grateful worship. I owe everything to him.

Bringing Grace and Good Works Together

How do we put the two sides together? Paul does just that in Ephesians 2:10. His bottom line—a believer is saved *for* good works not *by* good works. The prepositions make all the difference in the world. Let's look closer at how he knits faith and works.

Paul makes it crystal clear that God created us and saved us for a purpose. We are not an accident! No matter the circumstances of your birth, the failures and mistakes of your past, or your unfinished dreams for the future, your life has a purpose. God is at work! The Weaver's skill makes the masterpiece! *"For we are God's handiwork, created in Christ Jesus to do good works, which God prepared in advance for us to do"* (Eph 2:10).

The verse divides into four parts, each containing an important truth about our lives and their meaning.

"For We Are God's Handiwork..." This is quite a marvelous statement. The term "handiwork" is the Greek term from which our English word "poem" comes. The word describes something more than just a product. It is different from the term for "works" later in the verse. It's the word we have been pointing to throughout this study. The word carries the idea of handiwork, a work of art, a masterpiece! Can you picture a fine tapestry?

You are a creation of God. The Psalmist testifies, *"For you created my inmost being; you knit me together in my mother's womb. I praise you because I am fearfully and wonderfully made; your works are wonderful, I know that full well"* (Psalm 139: 13-14).

You are the crown of God's creation! Not everyone knows this. Imagine the emptiness and purposelessness of thinking that you are simply the product of some mindless explosion in the universe. What hope or direction can there be if we are nothing more than an evolutionary accident? No wonder much of our society is confused about the value of life, the meaning of marriage, and the very concept of right and wrong.

In that world of darkness, our text shines as a beacon of hope. "We are God's handiwork!" The next phrase raises the ante. *"Created in Christ Jesus."* This brings us to the heart of the verse. Ephesians 2 provides a wonder-filled explanation of our relationship with God. The chapter contrasts life before and after faith in Christ. *"As for you, you were dead in your transgressions and sins, in which you used to live when you followed the ways of this world. ... Like the rest, we were by nature objects of wrath"* (Ephesians 2:1-3).

That could be the end of the story. Many think it is. We live. We mess up our lives. We live with our messes. No second chances or "do-overs" allowed. Then we die. Period! For many, there are no other alternatives. But the Bible says otherwise. Ephesians 2:4-7 goes on to tell what God has done for us. God's purpose all along has been to make us part of his family through faith in Christ Jesus. He doesn't intend for sin and death to be the end. We are created by him and for him (Col 1:17). He put eternity in our hearts (Eccl 3:11). We are meant to enjoy God forever. That ultimate purpose can be discovered only through the grace experienced through faith in Jesus Christ.

The verse goes a step further. We are God's handiwork, created in Christ Jesus *"for good works."* The preceding verse makes it clear. We are not saved or rescued from sin by good works. Nothing we can do is good enough to outweigh the bad we do. We are saved by grace through faith! But we were created and saved for a purpose. God wants to use us for good.

A lot of people find the last part of the verse disturbing at first, *"which God prepared in advance for us to do."* In the opening verses of his letter, Paul says, "he chose us in him before the creation of the world" (1:4). It speaks of our "having been predestined according to the plan of him who works out everything in conformity with the purpose of his will" (1:11). To some that sounds like we are just pawns in some big chess game or gears in some cosmic machine. Maybe we are just puppets. God pulls our strings and we jump. Nothing could be further from the truth.

These words are simply affirming what Paul has been saying from the beginning of Ephesians. God is at work! He always has been—whether we always see it or not. He is weaving a masterpiece. He is always working on the topside of the tapestry. We live on the underside. If we are "in Christ," we know one thing for certain. Ultimately God is in control. He has created us with freedom and responsibility. But he has done so in a way that guarantees purpose and direction. He sets us free to face life with confidence and without fear. *"And we know that in all things God works for the good of those who love him, who have been called according to his purpose"* (Rm 8:28).

Life's No Accident!

"For we are God's handiwork, created in Christ Jesus for good works, which God prepared in advance for us to do." Grace and good works can never be separated. Both demonstrate that God is at work and that makes all the difference.

God Is Building a Church

God didn't save us to live life alone. He saved us for community and fellowship. That has always been a part of his plan. He has invested a lot to bring that about. He is especially interested in bringing people together who otherwise would have nothing to do with one another. Paul now turns to an explanation of that special work.

God's gracious plan touches our lives individually. But his plan (that grand tapestry he is weaving together largely unseen and unknown to us) is about more than us individually. His plan includes me, but it is not limited to me. His plan encompasses the work he is doing collectively in his people—the church, the community of faith. Most importantly, his plan (the weaving) didn't start with us. He began his work in eternity past, whether we can comprehend that or not. His work will continue into eternity future, long after we are gone.

What is this corporate plan? To bring everything together in Christ. *"He made known to us the mystery of his will according to his good pleasure, which he purposed in Christ, to be put into effect when the times reach their fulfillment—to bring unity to all things under Christ"* (Eph 1:9-10).   That will happen someday—in his perfect timing. But for now, he is at work providing a glimpse of what is to come by showing what he can do now through the unity of his church. We are his test plot, a living demonstration of his power and purpose. He is declaring to the world—"See what I am doing in my church. If I can do it there, I can do it anywhere." That's the burden of the last part of Ephesians 2.

God's Plan—One New Race

God's gracious goal was to create a new race of humanity—no longer Jew or Gentile, but one people made one in Christ—a third race, if you will. That means the hostility and rivalry must end. Both groups have the same access to God through the very same means—faith in the grace offering of Christ on the cross. No longer are there two groups, two paths, or two spiritual destinies. Through faith in Christ, the two have become one. Our task now is to act like it. Make it real for the world to see as a foretaste of what the Lord intends to do for anyone who embraces the gospel of Christ.

This truth certainly leaves no room for any kind of antisemitism among the followers of Christ. Sadly that has not always been the case. For example, late in life, Martin Luther allowed himself to sink into a miry pit of abusive words and attitudes toward all things Jewish. Was it old age or something more sinister catching up with the reformer? For all the good he did, Luther left a bitter legacy for some of his followers, something which Hitler's followers were glad to embrace. Christ's church should be a place of gratitude for its Hebrew legacy. It should be the last place anyone should ever find any kind of racial or ethnic bigotry. All of us are sinners in need of grace. All of us, Jew or non-Jew, can find new life and new beginnings through the Jewish Messiah. That is God's vision for the church.

The church—the community of Christ's saved people—must be a place where everything and everyone provides a living demonstration that the "ground at the foot of the cross" is level. We are "blood" brothers and sisters that nothing can separate. The blood of Jesus brought us together. As believers united by the cross, we must not let anything—race, nationality, class, rank, position, education, wealth, sectarian loyalties, on and on the list could go—become more defining of our relationships than our common faith in the sacrifice of Christ.

Paul's appeal for peace and unity makes one thing crystal clear— the church is vital. Paul does not envision individual believers floating around, each doing their own things and concerned only about their own personal likes and dislikes. Christ promised to build a church—a community of believing people who would stand together against the worst the enemy could throw at them.

The church rests on the shoulders of the apostles and prophets, those first-century servants through whom God revealed his plan and purpose. But the main thing was Jesus Christ. He was and is the cornerstone that holds everything together. The people committed to that message are where God is at work in the world. In a sense, God is present everywhere, but his presence and power are first experienced in the church. Any believer who wants to be used powerfully by God must somehow link arms with other like-minded believers. Every follower of Jesus needs other believers. That's where God is at work!

Paul now turns his attention to a fuller explanation of how the church, not some mystical, ideal church, but real, living congregations of believers, fits into God's eternal plan and the work he is doing in the world here and now. That's a big assignment. He will need to pray about that.

Chapter Four: Putting Hell on Notice

For this reason I, Paul, the prisoner of Christ Jesus for the sake of you Gentiles—Surely you have heard about the administration of God's grace that was given to me for you, that is, the mystery made known to me by revelation, as I have already written briefly. In reading this, then, you will be able to understand my insight into the mystery of Christ, which was not made known to people in other generations as it has now been revealed by the Spirit to God's holy apostles and prophets. This mystery is that through the gospel the Gentiles are heirs together with Israel, members together of one body, and sharers together in the promise in Christ Jesus. I became a servant of this gospel by the gift of God's grace given me through the working of his power. Although I am less than the least of all the Lord's people, this grace was given me: to preach to the Gentiles the boundless riches of Christ, and to make plain to everyone the administration of this mystery, which for ages past was kept hidden in God, who created all things. His intent was that now, through the church, the manifold wisdom of God should be made known to the rulers and authorities in the heavenly realms, according to his

Ephesians 3:1-13

There is more to the world we live in than what meets the eye. God is at work, and that changes everything. We may never understand the full scope of that reality apart from faith. "Faith is the evidence of things unseen..." (Heb 11:1). The Lord of our lives is weaving a marvelously beautiful tapestry around us, in us, and for us!

On the top side, the right side, of the weaving, everything comes into shape; on the underside, the back side, not so much. We occasionally see hints of beauty on the underside but nothing like what is coming into focus on the top. If only we could glimpse what the Weaver has in mind! That's the burden of Ephesians—to provide that glimpse!

So far, Paul has cast a vision for the eternal purpose of God and how it intersects with the life of a believer. Make no mistake about it; God is at work. He is far from finished. He has proved this over and over again, no less than when the believer was transformed by the gospel. That transformation reflects God's purpose. It is both individual and corporate. Individually, the believer moved from death to life, darkness to light. Corporately, the believer became part of a community of faith that transcends every racial, ethnic, and social barrier known to man. Demonstrating that in real life becomes a challenge so big and important that it will only happen when God brings it about in response to his people's prayers. That's where Paul goes next.

Ephesians as a Prayer Letter

Ephesians is a letter saturated with prayer. From beginning to end, Paul, the missionary, wants the Ephesian believers to pray for his ministry. But most importantly, he wants them to know that he is praying for them and their ministry to others in their city. Note the prayers embedded in the letter:

Chapter 1 begins with an attitude of prayer. The focus is on God, his goodness, and his graciousness toward his children. That's the atmosphere in which prayer flourishes—knowing who God is and what he has done. That he has already blessed us more than we know and has greater plans for us than we could possibly imagine. Without this picture of God's greatness, a believer has little incentive for prayer. Once the believer sees God in this light, he has no reason not to pray.

Chapter 1 ends with an actual prayer. Paul wants his readers to know the depth of his prayers for them. If only they could see their world the way God sees it, everything would change. That's his prayer-hope for them.

Chapter 3 begins with prayer but is quickly interrupted as Paul explains the foundation of his ministry. If his readers don't understand that, they won't understand his passion, his purpose, or much less his prayers. A few sentences later, Paul returns to his prayer. After hearing his heart, they are ready to hear his prayer. The apostle mines the riches of God's greatness as he prays for his readers. He yearns for the day they will grasp the magnitude of the gospel and faith's potential in their lives and church.

In Chapter 6, Paul closes his letter with a call to take the spiritual battle ahead seriously. The battle will call for their best. They need God's amour and a soldier's courage if they expect to be battle ready. But underneath the military talk lies a reliance on prayer. It is ultimately God's battle, not theirs. If they think they can fight with their strength, they are sadly mistaken. Only if they are "prayed up" can they expect to "stand up." Prayer is an essential, not a luxury, for battle readiness.

In Chapter 2, Paul explains the gospel of grace and its universal implications. God has one vision for one church built on Christ, grounded in grace, and composed of Jews and Gentiles alike. Only a united church can be the vehicle of the gospel for a world that desperately needs the good news of what Christ has done for them. A divided church with the unifying message of grace will never appeal to a divided world.

A lot is at stake. The church dare not fail. But fail it will if it fails in prayer. So Paul prays for the Gentile church. He is a Jew of Jews but is God's messenger for the non-Jew. He may have been born and raised a Jew, yet he was God's chosen messenger to take the gospel to the Gentiles.

The non-Jews have not replaced the Jews. They have joined the Jews who have come to faith in Jesus through the message of grace. They have a story that needs telling. And tell it they must. Paul invites them to join him in his gospel ministry. They are critical to what he is doing. That's why he prays for them and knows he needs them to pray for him.

Paul is a prisoner. But note how he describes his incarceration. Others may have thought that he was a "guest" of the empire. Roman soldiers took turns standing guard over him. He awaited Caesar's verdict. Only the emperor could determine his future. Or so it seemed. But Paul knew better! The King of kings, not the king of Rome or any other earthly monarch, was in control. Paul was a *prisoner of Jesus Christ.* Christ alone held the key to his future. Paul knew he would be a prisoner only as long as he served the Lord's purposes, not one minute longer.

Prayer Interrupted

Paul begins his prayer but then pauses. "For this reason, I bow my knees." He stops and won't pick up the prayer again until Verse 14. Perhaps, he realizes his readers won't understand or appreciate his prayer for their unity and mission ministry unless they understood his mission. Perhaps he was assuming too much about what they understood. So he pauses, takes a couple of steps back, and begins again at square one. His mission to reach non-Jews with the message of the Jewish Messiah was a God thing—first, last, and always.

He knows that his own coming to Christ and his mission to bring others to Christ began in the mind of God. Paul couldn't take credit for it. He could only praise God's grace. That brightened and affected everything he did. He was a steward, not the master. God saved him, put him on the road to the gospel, and opened every door Paul had ever walked through. This was the gospel *of God!*

Paul wouldn't have known what God was doing in the world if the God of heaven hadn't intercepted the trajectory of his life and set him on a new course. He calls it a mystery, a term that in scripture refers to something that can only be known by revelation, by an act of God. Long before Paul, men of God had tried to think through where God was leading his people and what his ultimate plan was. Some thought they had it figured out. Some gave up the search. But finally, God revealed the plan.

All along, God had intended that his plan was not about the Jews at all. Indeed, he had chosen the Jews for a special purpose, but that purpose wasn't what many had thought it was. It wasn't to reward the Jewish people. Rather, he was using the Jewish people to ultimately bless all people—Jews and Gentiles alike. Who would have thought that Abraham, Moses, David, the prophets, and everyone else in the Jewish scriptures were merely stepping stones that would finally lead to the Jewish Messiah, who would turn out to be the Savior of Jews AND Gentiles! Those who came to faith in Jesus were all part of the same body, the church of Jesus Christ.

The Overflow of Grace

Paul's ministry—every sermon he ever preached, every miracle he had ever been part of, and every church he had helped plant—was an overflow of God's grace. It was indeed a God thing! Paul insisted that he had no other explanation for why God had chosen him. He wasn't the brightest, the most eloquent, and the most skilled workman at God's disposal. Paul knew what God had taught from the very beginning. It was all of grace. No one, not even Paul, could claim credit. All the praise belonged to God alone! The message was about Jesus and him alone.

Note the powerful statement about the role of scripture in the life of a believer. Verse 4, "When you read this, you can perceive my insight into the mystery of Christ." Paul's letters, beyond just a personal correspondence between a missionary and the people he had brought to faith, are a deep dive into the will of God. By reading these words, anyone can understand what they would never otherwise know. We see beyond our side of the tapestry. We get a glimpse of the other side, God's eternal purpose.

If his Ephesian readers didn't grasp this work of grace, then they couldn't understand Paul's passion and prayers for them. He prayed for them because they were the tip of the spear. Their church—indeed, every local congregation—was the point of contact between God's gracious purpose and the enemies' opposition. Their congregation was the focal point where light and darkness met. They might have thought they were simply a small social group that met on the city's back streets to encourage one another in their newfound faith. They were that. But they were so much more. They were a key component in God's strategy for overcoming the forces of evil in a world gone wrong. Their church mattered because they were part of a battle bigger than themselves.

They were God's show and tell, a living and walking demonstration of what God wanted to do in every life. If he could do what he was doing in their lives, he could do it anywhere.

What is the purpose of the church? Paul puts it front and center in Verse 10, "so that through the church the manifold wisdom of God might be made known to the rulers and authorities in the heavenly places." *Authorities and powers* were Paul's terms for the unseen Satanic forces that worked behind the scenes, undermining the work of God and the gospel. We may not see them. We may not always understand them. Too often, we simply ignore them or assume they don't exist. We mistakenly think that our battle is against flesh and blood. If we only knew the real opposition we battle, we might take the conflict more seriously. At the very least, our tactics would change. Ultimately we would be forced to realize that the battle is the Lord's and not ours alone.

God's purpose for his people, the church, is not just to keep religious folk off the streets, cheer them up when they are down, and equip them to do a few good works along the way. Certainly, his purpose for the church is not to fight fire with fire, to be like and act like the world. His goal is not to prove that church members are better religious warriors than unchurched folk. God's aim is not for our church to be more politically powerful, bigger, richer, and more influential than anyone else. Ultimately it is not about us. It is about God's glory.

Putting Hell on Notice

The church is the evidence that the gospel is real and true. Through the church, God is putting hell on notice. The devil's days are numbered. Nothing that hell can do will stand against God's eternal plan. If God's will can reign supreme in the church, then it can overcome every bomb that hell can throw against it. The outcome of the spiritual battle has already been determined. The war is won. The church is proof.

What is God trying to prove through the church? Given Paul's emphasis on unity and interdependence throughout the rest of the letter, it seems clear that the church's purpose is to show what God can do when we turn control over to him. The church is living proof that God can change lives, bring people together, and turn enemies into coworkers. The church is a laboratory of love. Jesus said, *"They will know you are Christians by your love?"* (John 13:35). That's why he prayed that the church would be famous for its unity (Jn 17:21). Without that demonstration of love and unity, the world (outsiders) would have a right to conclude that the whole thing is a farce. No one would have any reason to believe that God could actually do what the gospel promised. God's eternal purpose is to point to the church and announce to the devil and all his henchmen, "See, I told you what can happen. Look at my church. What I did for them I can do anywhere in anybody who turns their lives over to me."

God's Demonstration Plot

In the center of the modern University of Illinois campus in Urbana stands a small, seemingly out-of-place garden plot. It is not decorative or ornamental. It is the site of one of the longest, ongoing, carefully monitored scientific agricultural experiments in the world. The Morrow Plots have occupied that same piece of ground since 1876. The campus has grown up around it.

Each year, scientists monitor and sample the soil, plant, fertilize, and water the crop. They record weather conditions, rainfall, and any insect infestations. When the crop is harvested in the fall, they measure the results, compare one variety of seeds with another, and carefully identify any significant scientific insights. They have been recording the results from that same patch of ground for 150 years! The goal is to develop better hybrids and cultivation methods that can be translated into actual practices on working farms.

The Morrow Plots are small, less than a single acre. The harvest wouldn't amount to much in the grand scheme of things. It is not intended to. They are an experiment, a demonstration. The researchers have set out to show what can be done in a small controllable sample. They then develop tools and processes that can be projected onto a much larger scale. When they publish the outcomes, they are saying, "If this works here, then it can work elsewhere as well."

That's the church! Each small local congregation is God's demonstration plot. What he does in that one spot can be multiplied across town and around the globe. But it is not just about developing betters methods of church growth. Some church growth discussions are valid and needed. But God's goal is greater than growth. He wants to declare to the "powers that be" his greatness and goodness. The church, each church, is intended to be a living demonstration that proves what God is capable of doing. Few will believe in the power of God and his ability to bless and transform lives until they see it lived out in the marriages, families, and churches of the communities they know. The church is proof positive that the gospel is not just theoretical. It "works" every time it is preached and believed because God is at work. When the church starts really believing, loving, and walking in unity, hell trembles!

God Is Still At Work!

Why does Paul interrupt his prayer to make this point? The folk in this young church that he had planted a few years before need encouragement. They face great opposition in their community. They have only recently learned that Paul has been arrested and may well be executed. They could easily become disillusioned. He wants them to be bold even in the midst of such stressful circumstances. "Don't lose heart," he insists. "I haven't! God is greater than any of the challenges we face. He has a greater purpose for each of us. I may be suffering some setbacks right now, but our God is still on the throne. He is still in control. No matter how confusing this side of the tapestry may look right now, don't forget the other side. The Master Weaver is still at work!"

Paul's concern is that his friends will "lose heart" when they learn of his struggles. That's the last thing he wants. That's why he prays for them. "Lose heart" is a metaphor for the loss of courage or discouragement, a temptation to give up or turn back. Losing heart is the opposite of keeping the faith, standing tall, or living with eternity in mind. The phrase is used several times in our English translations of the New Testament.

In Luke 18:1, Jesus calls for his disciples to pray and not lose heart. Here the actual term refers to "acting badly" or giving in to whatever is opposing us. Prayer is always an alternative to giving up. Prayer has always been a powerful "resistance" movement.

Paul uses the same expression in 2 Corinthian 4:1 when he insists that his ministry of reconciliation encourages him to never "lose heart." Giving up would mean turning to underhanded and deceptive means to advance the gospel. A few verses later, he admits that physically he grows weary (4:16). His outer man is wasting away, but spiritually he remains strong. He faces great opposition, but he doesn't give up.

In his concluding words to the Galatians, Paul challenges his readers to never give up or grow weary when doing good (6:9). They will reap a harvest in God's time. That's a guarantee. They have every reason to keep on keeping on!

Paul uses a different Greek term in Colossians 3:21 when he challenges fathers to deal gently with their children. Otherwise, they could frustrate and embitter their young.   That, in turn, could lead them to lose heart. This term describes what happens when someone loses their passion or eagerness. They may still go through the motions, but the heart is no longer in it.

The writer of Hebrews (12:3) uses yet another expression when he exhorts his readers to keep their eyes on Jesus, who endured horrible suffering at the hands of sinners on the cross. His example provides an incentive to keep the faith. He wants his readers not to grow weary or lose heart. Here the phrase translates to "growing weak or sick in soul."   Strength in the inner man provides the antidote to giving up.

That's Paul's concern. He worries that his friends will be discouraged and lose their zeal for the work of God. A disheartened church easily becomes an ineffective church. That can't happen. Their calling is too important. This is why he prays.

Chapter Five: Radical Praying

For this reason I kneel before the Father, from whom every family in heaven and on earth derives its name. I pray that out of his glorious riches he may strengthen you with power through his Spirit in your inner being, so that Christ may dwell in your hearts through faith. And I pray that you, being rooted and established in love, may have power, together with all the Lord's holy people, to grasp how wide and long and high and deep is the love of Christ, and to know this love that surpasses knowledge—that you may be filled to the measure of all the fullness of God. Now to him who is able to do immeasurably more than all we ask or imagine, according to his power that is at work within us, to him be glory in the church and in Christ Jesus throughout all generations, for ever and ever! Amen.

Ephesians 3:14-21

Reading Paul's letter to Ephesians reminds me of driving in Alaska. I've visited the Last Frontier many times. In fact, I lived in Anchorage for a year, not long ago. But no matter how many times I've explored that vast wilderness, my reaction is always the same. I specifically remember driving into the little tourist village of Talkeetna. The town's claim to fame is that it is the closest settlement to Denali National Park and the jumping-off point for many mountain climbers who attempt to scale the highest peak in North America each year.

After the two-hour drive north from Alaska's biggest city, I am always numb from sensory overload. No matter which direction I look from the Parks Highway, I can see huge mountain ranges that seem to never end. Every scene is more breathtaking than the one before. Just when I think I couldn't possibly see anything more amazing, the two-lane blacktop makes a sharp turn, and there it is! Denali! The monster mountain (20,310 feet) dwarfs all the other peaks by comparison. Its snow-laden slopes loom above the landscape. Still over fifty miles away, "The Great One" seems like I could reach out and touch it.

The beginning chapters of Ephesians read like that wilderness drive. Paul takes us on an unbelievably rich journey. He paints one glorious word picture after another. He unveils scenes of God's glory and grace, his purpose and plan for those in Christ, and the transforming power of the gospel in any life that will come to him in faith. He calls the church to the great task of reflecting God's glory for not only the world to see but also for "rulers and authorities in heavenly places" to witness (3:10). Just when I think I couldn't come across anything more amazing, I turn the corner, and there it is!

This isn't just any prayer. Paul unleashes one of the most radical prayers found anywhere. He has been leading up to it since the beginning of the letter. The prayer in Chapter 1 (1:15-23) provided a prelude. Now he pulls out all the stops. The prayer is intentionally a turning point in the letter. In the prayer, Paul brings together the themes he has already written. He also lays the foundation for the way of life he will outline in the rest of the book. The content of the prayer is no accident.

The prayer is "radical" in that it goes to the root of what praying has always been about. That's the original meaning of the term "radical." "Radical" means, in its basic form, to go to the root or foundation of something. In this prayer, Paul takes us back to the fundamental issues of the faith and what it means to pray. He approaches prayer not as a personal retreat into comfort and safety but as a call to live God's eternal purpose. For Paul, prayer is not about making ourselves feel better but about preparing for battle. This radical prayer assumes that God is at work and calls upon him to do his work in us and through us.

How We Learn to Pray

We learn to pray in many ways, mostly by doing it. But beyond that, most of what we know about prayer and how we pray, we learned at the feet of our mentors. Consciously or otherwise, we hear the prayers of people we respect and gradually mimic them. I can remember my grandfather's prayers at the dinner table and those of the respected elders at the communion table in my childhood church. Over time, their phrases and priorities began to shape my prayers.

That's the premise behind the Lord's Prayer. The disciples had seen Jesus pray often enough. They no doubt were impressed by what they witnessed. Maybe they had heard his words or maybe they hadn't. They wanted more. They asked him to teach them to pray. I am sure they already understood the importance of prayer. They wanted him to teach them *how* to pray. Perhaps they were looking for a magic formula, some mantra that would guarantee that what they prayed for they would receive. If that was what they were looking for, I am sure they were disappointed. What he provided was simple, almost childlike. He offered no secret ritual, just a simple, straightforward conversation with the Heavenly Father. Most of all, he taught them *to pray.* The Father was eagerly waiting to hear from them.

"For this reason"—the opening phrase appears twice when Paul starts and pauses and then again when he begins. The second, "for this reason" (3:14), follows an explanation of the church's global, or even bigger—"cosmic"—mission. The church's living exhibition of the gospel's ability to bring people together provides evidence of the power of God's grace. The world will only believe God's love is real when they see it in the church. God's reputation is at stake.

Praying to Our Father

Next, Paul exposes the radical manner of his prayer. "I kneel before the Father." We may pray in many postures, but radical prayer requires one basic attitude. Standing with heads bowed, prostrating, or sitting quietly are all appropriate. But never, ever dare we pray in pride. We are never demanding as if we could tell God what to do. We are asking. We are submitting. Fear and trembling are always the approach of a praying person who knows whom they are approaching.

Paul describes his God as "the Father, from whom every family in heaven and on earth derives its name." We have no exclusive claim on God. He is not ours only. He is bigger than our tribe, clan, or nation. The Father who hears our prayers is available to anyone and everyone who comes to him in faith. His blessings and love flow far wider and deeper than our personal concerns. If that doesn't affect our perspective in prayer, nothing will. He is the one who defines our identity. He is our source. He has every right to rule over us.

If there is a sense in which he is Father of all, then we cannot pray as if we alone have a right to ask for his blessings. It is not an us versus them when we pray. He loves "them" just as much as he loves me. Our prayer should reflect that larger vision. He is never just "my" Father. That needs to be settled before we pray.

This priority affects how we pray and what we pray for. We seek his glory, not our own. We want *his* kingdom to expand, not our *personal* kingdoms. Whatever the outcome of our requests, it will flow from his abundance, not our achievement. We don't earn his favor. Whatever favor we receive flows from the "riches of his glory." His favor flows from his character, not ours. We receive from the overflow of his grace.

Above all, our goal is to bring him glory "in the church and in Christ Jesus." Praying is never about us. It is always about him. Nor are our prayers limited to our problems and dreams. Like Paul, we pray visionary prayers. We are thinking about "all generations," both for time and eternity. Radical praying never settles for anything less than a radical view of God.

A Radical Prayer List

Next, Paul's prayer turns to his petition, what he desires God to do in the lives of his readers. He asks the Father to grant three overlapping blessings. Perhaps most striking is what he doesn't ask for. He doesn't ask for wealth or health, protection from hard times, or easier lives. Paul's prayer list doesn't read like the admittance registry at the Ephesian General Hospital. Praying for the sick and the hurting is always good and proper. But if that is the total sum and substance of our petitions, we have missed the heart of God. We can pray for things near and dear to us, but radical praying never omits the things near and dear to the Father.

Paul focuses on God's eternal purpose for his people by asking for inner strength, understanding what it means to truly love one another. Underneath each petition is the desire that these believers learn to appreciate that God is weaving something in their lives, even though they may not be able to see the outcome—yet! What he weaves is not nearly as important as the fact that He God is the one weaving it. When they understand that "God is at work," they will find rest in their faith. Regardless of what they are experiencing at any given moment, they will not "lose heart" but stand firm in the conviction that God has everything under control.

Inside Out Faith

Paul's first concern is for their inner strength. If they are strong on the inside, they can survive anything on the outside. That doesn't mean the outside doesn't matter. Our inner belief finds expression in our outer behavior. Both are vital. For most of us, the outer can easily overshadow the inner. That's part of the human condition. The creator forever brought the two together when the "word became flesh" (Jn 1:14). The reality remains—if the inner is weak, the outer "man" will be pushed and squeezed by whatever outside force seems stronger at the moment.

Secondly, Paul prays that the lives of Christian friends might overflow with love. He wants them to be saturated with love (rooted and established). He looks forward to a day when they will have the power to comprehend how big God's love really is. It is one thing to talk about love; it is another to truly understand what that means for our relationships and perspectives in the church. Talking about loving and actually loving are two different things.

If we know we are loved, we can risk loving others, even those who are totally different from us. That's why Paul prays that his readers, and us by extension, can grasp "how wide and long and high and deep is the love of Christ." *Wide* may picture the broad, all-inclusive love that encircles people groups across the geographic and cultural divides that we would seldom think to cross but for the message of grace found in Jesus. *Long* could describe the unending, eternal nature of his love. The gospel has no "use by" or expiration date. We can't outlive or stand by waiting for the clock to run out. He loves now and forever. Could *high* cover those exciting, wonder-filled experiences of the Christian life? When everything is going well, it is all too easy to want to stay there, focus inward, and never let go of the good times. But high love is no less sharing love. *Deep* might be the valley experiences, the harder and darker times. Understanding God's love even when the hard times come keeps us from retreating into our shells, trying to protect ourselves from more pain and hurts. Those low moments are the very moments we need to lean on the love of our brothers and sisters.

Such a love surely passes understanding. We will never fully define it or explain it, but we can live it and share it "with all the Lord's people." Such love must be discovered in community, in fellowship with other believers. It will never be known alone.

Filled With the Fullness of God

In his third and final petition, Paul asks that his readers might be filled to the measure of the fullness of God. Christ dwelling in our hearts, being rooted in love, and being filled with God's fullness all express the same conviction. God is at work in our world and our lives. He is not a God of "once upon a time." He didn't retire when the last apostle died. Nor is he a God who limits his work to the pages of a holy book. He reveals himself in the pages of scripture. No doubt about that! But that's not all of his work. He is still "able to do immeasurably more than we ask or imagine." Paul's radical pray assumes the radical reality of God.

The ending benediction provides the big, shiny bow that puts the final touch on the majestic prayer. This prayer, all prayer, rests on the reality of God's greatness. He is able. If he isn't, then prayer makes no sense. His ability, not our ability, provides prayer's potential. His ability surpasses ours in ways that defy description. Understand him or not, our great God is at work in and around us. That's what we are depending on. We pray because we want his honor and glory exalted. "Thy kingdom come; thy will be done." That's what we pray for. We want the church to be the place where he is known and praised. We want Jesus lifted up and praised. We desire everyone who comes after us to know what he has done for us and in us. That's our forever prayer. God's eternal purpose is our eternal prayer!

What If God Has Left the Building?

What would happen if God abandoned the church? What if God is no longer at work? Would anybody even notice? A. W. Tozer suggested probably not. The great devotional author is reported to have said, "If God were to take the Holy Spirit out of this world, much of what the church is doing would go right on; and nobody would know the difference." Someone else has observed, "When the early church fathers came together, they talked about their powers. When modern church men gather, they speak of their problems."

What would happen if we began to pray Paul's radical prayer? What would it look like if the church you know best really expected God to work? I suspect a great many things would change. The closing doxology of Paul's prayer provides more than a few clues.

Lord, Give Me a Daring Church

If God showed up with power in many of our churches today, the first thing that would happen is that lot of people would have a heart attack. Immediately after that, the deacons would call a board meeting and vote that things return to how they were. Seriously, many of us wouldn't know what to do if God suddenly shook things up. We have become comfortable with normal. We like predictability. God's power might threaten that. Maybe we need to be threatened!

A powerful church would be a more daring church. Hope would reign. Faith would replace fear. People would see possibilities where they had only seen problems. The most cautious and pessimistic voices would no longer rule the day.

The power to dare stands in stark contrast with self-confidence. Daring faith is God-confidence. It marks a people who are passionate about the purposes of God. Their own goals and dreams take second place. When God's presence and purpose are front and center, God's power flows freely.

Too many churches are like what John Bisagno said his church used to be like. John Bisagno, a former pastor of Houston's First Baptist Church, tells the story of his initial interview for the position of pastor of the church he would eventually serve for many years. He describes entering the church's auditorium. It was dimly lit. A small group of people huddled together near the front. He recalled that the congregation was singing some "old slow funeral type song" that filled the room with notes of discouragement and depression. Bisagno was not impressed.

Later that day, he took a walk in downtown Houston to get a feel for the neighborhood surrounding the church. As he passed a jewelry store, he noticed it appeared to be having some sort of grand opening. Bright lights sparkled over the entry. A smiling greeter stood on duty at the door to welcome customers. Inside, the sounds of cheerful music played in the background. A crowd of customers and salespeople shared refreshments. In every direction he looked, he could see people having a good time talking and laughing with each other. Someone welcomed him, offered him some punch, and encouraged him to join the celebration.

Bisagno thought about his two experiences at the church and the jewelry store. He later said that after attending both, if the store had offered an invitation, he would have joined the jewelry store!

Lord, Give Me a Caring Church

If God responded to our radical praying and showed up in power, another change would quickly follow. The result would be a more caring church. That theme flows throughout Paul's prayer.

On August 6, 1945, at precisely 8:15 AM, a uranium bomb exploded over the Japanese city of Hiroshima. Within seconds, the entire city lay in ruins. Seventy thousand people were dead and another seventy thousand seriously injured. That one bomb had exploded with a force greater than twenty thousand tons of TNT. That is power!

But that is not the only power. For five years, I could look out my office window and view a small nuclear reactor adjacent to our university's research facility. The very same principles of physics that made possible the atomic bomb were at work in that reactor and were used to generate electricity for huge cities. When the reactor operates properly, no one hears an explosion. Nobody witnesses the telltale mushroom cloud. No neighbors are put in danger. But there is power! A reactor's power may be quiet and not nearly as spectacular as a bomb, but it is power nonetheless. In fact, the silent energy of that reactor can be far more powerful and certainly more significant than the force of a thousand bombs.

Clearly, real power need not be spectacular, violent, or even visible. Perhaps the greatest power needed by many churches is not the ability to work miracles but the power to love one another. More than we need the force of the Spirit, we need the fruit of the Spirit (Gal 5:22-23). Power, even miraculous power, can never replace the powerful demonstration of love for one another (1 Cor 13:1-3).

Lord, Give Me a Sharing Church

If the church prayed like Paul, it would become more daring. It would look beyond itself and become more caring. Radical praying would also result in a work of God that would create a sharing church. Sharing, the radical giving away of ourselves and our faith to others is a message our needy world desperately needs to hear. That was the power Jesus promised his disciples as he departed this world for the one above. *"You will receive power when the Holy Spirit comes upon you and you will be my witnesses…"* (Acts 1:8).

That is exactly what happened on Pentecost. The Spirit came. The followers of Jesus were filled with the powerful presence of the Holy Spirit. They proclaimed the gospel of Jesus. Thousands came to know Christ. That's the power to share.

When that power came, Jesus was lifted up. The focus was on what he had done. The message wasn't about the church or what people needed to do for God. It was all about what the God of heaven had done for them in Christ Jesus. The witness was not about the Spirit, but about the crucified and resurrected Christ. Those Spirit-powered believers couldn't stop talking about Jesus. They shared his message across the street, across cultural and social barriers, and across generations. Their confidence didn't rest in themselves but in the Lord who was at work in them.

That is still true. As we stand up, speak up, and live up for Christ, we have the absolute assurance that we are not alone. A church at work in the harvest is part of the great co-mission. It is not operating on its own power. God is at work!

Chapter Six: Living Like Heaven on Earth

As a prisoner for the Lord, then, I urge you to live a life worthy of the calling you have received. Be completely humble and gentle; be patient, bearing with one another in love. Make every effort to keep the unity of the Spirit through the bond of peace. There is one body and one Spirit, just as you were called to one hope when you were called; one Lord, one faith, one baptism; one God and Father of all, who is over all and through all and in all.

Ephesians 4:1-6

Imagine walking into a dark room with no lights, no windows, total darkness. You stumble around, bumping into tables, knocking over this item or that item at every turn. You receive a few bumps and bruises along the way. You stub your toe on who knows what. But then, suppose somebody turns on a light for just a bit. The room is suddenly as bright as day. You can see it all—once your eyes adjust. You take it all in and then just as quickly as the light came on, it is off. Darkness again!

Even though you are still in the dark room, the situation has changed. Even if it were only for a few seconds, you saw what was ahead of you. You might still stumble and bump into a few things, but not like before. Now you know what's in the room. Of course, you probably don't remember everything. But now you have an idea where you are and where you are headed.

That's where we are at in Ephesians. Paul has turned the light on. He has explained what the Weaver is up to. The Master has a plan and now you have had an opportunity to catch a brief glimpse of it. You may still be living on the underside of life, but now you know what it is all about. "Therefore—then"—what is your next step? We are at a major transition in Ephesians.

Paul again reminds them where he is. *As a prisoner!* However tough their situation is or may become, it is likely not nearly as dire as his. He may be a prisoner, but he knows who is in control. The authorities had Paul under lock and key, but he knew the Weaver. His jailers only thought they had him imprisoned. He knew his fate was actually in the hands of someone much more powerful than any mere Roman emperor. He was right where the Lord wanted him. He would be there not one minute longer than what the Lord intended.

Walking Like a Christian

The word for "*live*" in the phrase "*live a life worthy of the calling*" is actually a term that can be translated as "w*alk*." This is a common metaphor for life. It pictures the Christian experience as a journey. Our surroundings may change. Fellow travelers may come and go. Sometimes the path is uphill and sometimes down. But the direction remains the same. We are following the course laid out for us. We are answering the "upward call" (Phil. 3:14).

Paul uses this image numerous times in Ephesians. Earlier, he had referred to the old life of sin as walking according to the world (2:2). But God changed our direction when he made us alive with Christ.

Now we walk a new path. We walk in pursuit of the good works for which our God has created us (2:10). As new creations, we can no longer be satisfied to walk as we once did or as those ignorant of God's purpose still do (4:17). Instead we follow the ways of God and walk in love as Christ did (5:2). We once may have walked in darkness, but no longer. Now we walk as children of the light (5:8). We live in a foolish world where men and women care little about how they live or where they are headed. But we are different. Our God has changed us. We care where we are headed and how we walk (5:15). We have a new direction and a new purpose.

We know that whatever we are and wherever we are headed is not our doing. We can never take credit for it. It is, we now know, all of grace. We have nothing to boast about. All the credit goes to him, who is fashioning something for us we could never make of ourselves. The Master Weaver deserves all the credit. To describe our lives as a calling means where we are or where we are headed is only by invitation. We were totally lost until we heard a voice out of the darkness, "This way! Just follow my voice and we'll get through this." We will find our way out, not by our own cleverness, but only by following the voice of the one who calls us.

What does a worthy walk (life) look like? On the one hand, we might be tempted to think of it in royal, majestic terms. A worthy walk might be pictured with a head held high, reflecting a status of superiority and aloofness. To think that way would be to forget the one we are following. A worthy walk is meant to mirror the life and character of our Lord and Savior, Jesus Christ. In every respect, such a life is just the opposite of what might otherwise be expected in normal life. We live on the underside. Our eyes are focused on the other side. But more than that, our eyes are on the Weaver and his eternal plan.

Paul stacks a series of characteristics on top of one another, each describing the quality of the worthy, called life. Together they form a snapshot of the Christ-like life, a life much different from what might be expected but exactly what is required of a life that fulfills God's eternal purpose for his people.

Gentleness goes hand in hand with humility. When we think too highly of ourselves, we tend to think little of others. We react to others with anger and rudeness because we think that's all they deserve. We expect them to treat us as their betters which we think we are. Paul links the terms in the parallel passage in Colossians— *"Therefore, as God's chosen people, holy and dearly loved, clothe yourselves with compassion, kindness, humility, gentleness and patience. Bear with each other and forgive one another if any of you has a grievance against someone. Forgive as the Lord forgave you. And over all these virtues put on love, which binds them all together in perfect unity"* (Col 3:12-14).

Patience carries the picture a step further. A worthy walk holds back. It doesn't boil over in anger or resentment at others. It seeks to see the best in how others treat us. It doesn't magnify the small slights and turn them into a justification for an angry response. The twin descriptor moves the attitude forward—"bearing with one another in love." This is more than tolerance. It is forgiveness in action. We live that way because we have come to understand that this is exactly how our God has treated us. How could we do less?

The capstone comes with the final phrase—*"make every effort to maintain the unity of the Spirit in the bond of peace."* This describes an attitude of eagerness. We don't just reluctantly tread this path, going someplace we really don't want to go. We want God's eternal goal of unity exhibited in his church because we have seen his vision. We want that life here and now. The unity we desire, we realize, is not of our making. He has already created it. We can't make it happen. We can only maintain what he has already fashioned. He has reconciled us through the cross. We enjoy peace with him and with all who are likewise reconciled to him. That is what binds us together.

Unity presupposes a basic level of agreement. As Amos puts it, *"Can two walk together unless they agree"* (3:3). Where do we start when we are trying to build like-mindedness in a Christian community? First, we need to agree to disagree. We must acknowledge that not everything is of equal importance. We will have personal opinions and preferences that don't have to be the same from person to person. We will have different experiences, backgrounds, and levels of knowledge that aren't alike. "In essentials unity, in opinions liberty, and in all things, love" is an old principle that makes all the difference. But even that is easier said than done. A few of us tend to see everything as essential. "If it is my opinion, then it ought to be your opinion as well. After all, if it wasn't right, it wouldn't be my opinion." Really?

The Glue that Holds Us Together

What is the glue that binds believers together in unity? The virtues in Verses 1-7 are what maintain it. Their absence will destroy it in the blink of an eye. But no amount of effort can create it where it doesn't already exist. Real unity grows from shared identity, the conviction that we belong together and are headed in the same direction and need one another. That is the essence of the *Seven Ones* of Verses 4-6. In a sense, these verses claim that these seven realities are the substance of our unity as believers. Two people who do not share these base convictions are not united, regardless of what else is true. People who share them will unite even if everything else in their lives is totally different.

Consider what Paul could have said but didn't. Real unity doesn't flow from the fact that we speak the same language or share the same national heritage or racial profile. It doesn't depend on our socio-economic status, our educational pedigree, or political preferences. It is not based on our likes and dislikes regarding church architecture or music. Oops—maybe I just went too far!

All of that is insignificant in comparison to our shared identity as followers of Jesus Christ. It is not the shape of the particular piece of the underside of the tapestry we share that binds us together but our conviction that it is the other side, the upper side that defines us. A lot of things on this side may divide us. We are united by what we believe about the other side.

Here We Stand Together

Paul lists seven theological categories, ideas, or doctrines. Typically, to the Hebrew mind, seven represented completeness and totality. In all likelihood, he wasn't claiming that these were the only things that matter, the sum total of Christian doctrine. But these seven provided an appropriate summary. These provided the common denominators that linked believers, regardless of whatever differences may otherwise exist.

Some historians see in this list an early creed of sorts. These were the sort of convictions to which most Christians could point and declare, "That's what we are all about." But even at that, these are broad categories that are largely undefined. It is when we try to micromanage the terms that we get into trouble. Paul lets them be. He simply states them and moves on.

Father, Son, and Spirit

Clearly, the list is trinitarian—one Spirit, one Lord, one God and Father. But even here, this falls short of a detailed explanation of what we mean by the Trinity. Theologians have argued about that for two thousand years plus. Perhaps we should leave this topic where the Bible leaves it—God, who is One, has revealed himself as Father, Son, and Holy Spirit. This is not three Gods but One. The oneness and threeness have existed from all eternity. If there is a difference, it is in emphasis. In the Father, the focus is on the authority and transcendence of God. The Son emphasizes the revelation of God in flesh and history. The Spirit centers on the invisible but personal and powerful presence of God with us. When we go beyond this, as well-intentioned as it may be, we too often paint ourselves into a corner. Going beyond God's self-revelation seldom proves helpful.

The structure of the *Seven Ones* comes in three triplets. The first focuses on the Spirit, the second on the Son (Paul uses the term Lord), and the third on the Father. He mentioned each in separate categories, yet they are bound together in an inseparable trio. For Paul, that was enough said!

The order of the *Seven Ones* may or may not be important. But having said that, there is a distinct flow. Paul starts with our present experience—one body, one Spirit, one hope of our calling. He moves to our conversion experience, the turning point from our past that brought us to where we are—one Lord, one faith, one baptism. He concludes by pointing to the sovereignty of the Father, who ties it all together. We are brothers and sisters because we have the same Father. We are family.

One Body—Many Parts

We are one body, a metaphor that will continue to be developed by Paul here and in other places (1 Corinthians 12 and Romans 12). Together we are the manifestation of the risen Christ in this world here and now. None of us by ourselves is the whole body, only parts. But we need the rest to be whole. It is the Spirit's presence that makes the church the body of Christ. Without the Spirit, the church is just another human organization. When the Spirit directs the body, the whole is greater than the sum of the parts. As believers in community, we demonstrate to a watching world the wisdom and glory of God (Eph 3:10). Our oneness flows from our common purpose and calling. We are united because we share a common destiny.

How did we come to share this calling? All of us, Jew or Gentile, male or female, rich or poor—add whatever human category you wish—came to be part of Christ's body through one faith, one Lord, one baptism. Faith can be objective or subjective. Objective faith refers to the content of our belief—the gospel revealed in Jesus Christ. Subjective faith highlights our belief or trust in that message. What Paul means (objective or subjective faith) is probably irrelevant. When we come to Christ, both are involved. The heart of the gospel (our faith) is Jesus—who he is and what he did. Other convictions may be important, but none are more important than our relationship with Christ.

Most likely, one baptism refers to the initiation rite into the Christian life. Baptism marks the point of separation from what we were to what we are in Christ. Paul describes it as dying and rising (Romans 6). Our unity is grounded in the reality of that transformation. One faith describes the message we accepted. One Lord is the one at the center of that message. One baptism marks the point in time when that became real in our experience.

One God and Father

All of this is tied together by the reality of the Heavenly Father's power and presence in our lives. An appeal to the Father's sovereign reign ebbs and flows throughout Ephesians. Paul begins by praising the Father of our Lord Jesus Christ, who blessed us in Christ with spiritual blessings (1:3). He prays that the Father of glory would give us the Spirit of wisdom and revelation (1:17). Later, he insists that we have access through Christ to the Father in the one Spirit (2:18). His prayer is to the Father from whom every family in heaven and earth is named (3:14). Finally, he reminds us that our worship is to always be filled with thanksgiving to God the

Father in the name of Christ for everything (5:20). The realization that we together share the loving, caring protection of our Father in Heaven is never far from the apostle's thinking.

This one God revealed himself in Christ. That became real in us through the Spirit. We belong to him. Our relationship with him defines who we are. If that is true—our identity is in Him, nothing being more important, then all of us who share that common relationship are one. Nothing should divide us. Nothing should be so important that it comes between us. We are one!

Now Paul turns to another essential ingredient of real unity.

Chapter Seven: Body Builders Needed

But to each one of us grace has been given as Christ apportioned it. This is why it says: "When he ascended on high, he took many captives and gave gifts to his people." (What does "he ascended" mean except that he also descended to the lower, earthly regions? He who descended is the very one who ascended higher than all the heavens, in order to fill the whole universe.) So Christ himself gave the apostles, the prophets, the evangelists, the pastors and teachers, to equip his people for works of service, so that the body of Christ may be built up until we all reach unity in the faith and in the knowledge of the Son of God and become mature, attaining to the whole measure of the fullness of Christ. Then we will no longer be infants, tossed back and forth by the waves, and blown here and there by every wind of teaching and by the cunning and craftiness of people in their deceitful scheming. Instead, speaking the truth in love, we will grow to become in every respect the mature body of him who is the head, that is, Christ. From him the whole body, joined and held together by every

*supporting ligament, grows and builds itself up in love,
as each part does its work.*

Ephesians 4:7-16

Christian unity matters. It is a reflection of the character and priorities of God. Unity glorifies God; disunity dishonors him. Furthermore, few unbelievers are likely to show much interest in a God whose followers can't get along. Such unity flows from the harmonious treatment of one another in practical personal relationships (vss. 1-3). That lifestyle of peace builds on the shared convictions of a common faith (vss. 4-6). We cannot walk together if we aren't in basic agreement about the beliefs that hold us together. But even that is seldom enough.

Perhaps we can understand our need and God's provision if we picture a symphony orchestra or large musical chorus. Many different people with many different potential contributions make up an orchestra. Strings, brass, percussion, woodwinds, and perhaps a few other assorted instruments come together to make the whole. All are needed. None are enough by themselves. Remember the elementary school band at its first performance. That's a sound only a parent can love and not always them. Or consider the cacophony of noise coming from even a celebrated orchestra tuning up!

A pleasing sound only results from the vast, diversified group coming together. For that to happen, two additional items are needed. First, they need to play the same music. One section can't play one song while another tries joining in with a totally different score. If we were thinking of congregational worship service, we might say they all need to be singing from the same hymnbook and the same page. I have witnessed services where that wasn't the case!

Every Symphony Needs a Conductor

In addition to the same musical score, our orchestra needs one more thing. They need a conductor. The conductor seldom plays an instrument. Yet his/her role is every bit as critical, even more so, as anyone else in the symphony. The conductor keeps the musicians together. He marks the timing. He helps the different groups know when to play and when to remain silent. In many cases, the conductor also serves as a teacher, helping to mentor and coach the various members of the orchestra. The more immature the musicians are, the more critical the teaching role of the conductor. The conductor sets the pace and keeps the diverse instruments moving together. With the same music and all eyes on the conductor, the musicians can work together to form a unified, pleasing sound.

If a church/congregation is a symphony with members playing different instruments, our convictions (the *Seven Ones* of vss. 4-6) form the score we play. Our leaders become the conductors that enable such diversity to come together into a unified and pleasing whole that makes the Christian experience a joy, advances the gospel, and glorifies our God. This is what Paul seeks to explain next.

In Ephesians and Colossians, Paul uses the metaphor of the body to underscore the Lordship of Christ as the head. "*And God placed all things under his feet and appointed him to be head over everything for the church, which is his body, the fullness of him who fills everything in every way*" (Eph 1:22-23). He focuses on the wholeness of the body under the direction of the head, the head being the singular part from which the whole body takes its identity and receives direction.

The Giver of Gifts

Paul appeals to the oneness of the body in Ephesians 4. As the people of God, we are connected. We have one identity and one direction. Yet unity does not mean uniformity. *"But to each one"*— a major challenge to unity is our diversity. We are not alike, nor were we intended to be. *"Grace has been given as Christ apportioned it..."* (Eph 4:7). Our Lord is in control. We differ because that's the way he made us. Or in this case, our abilities and contributions to the whole are not the same. But perhaps most importantly, it is all of grace. He didn't give "more" to some because they deserved it. What they received could not be interpreted as a reward for previous achievement. He gave what he wanted and gave out of grace. That fact should preclude the possibility of any prideful claim that I am better than you. The only one who can claim to be better is the giver and decider. The rest of us are simply "blessed."

To reinforce or perhaps illustrate this God-given diversity, Paul quotes Psalm 68:18. His quotation pictures a king coming home from battle to distribute the plunder of conquest to his subjects. As a result of the victory on the cross and in the resurrection, the ascended Christ has gifted his people. He descended in his incarnation, his birth, and earthly ministry. He arose in victory over sin and the devil. The glorified Christ then gifted his followers.

Different On Purpose!

It is important to note that this discussion of gifts, body-life, and interdependence differs in its emphasis from the others in the New Testament (1 Corinthians 12; Romans 12; 1 Peter 4). In these other places, Paul underscores the diversity the Lord has built into the church (his body). Each part needs the others. Pride or shame based on comparisons has no place. If we accept the Lordship of Christ, we must accept his decisions regarding the distribution of "gifts" to his people. The call is to love and serve one another to the best of our abilities. What others do is irrelevant to our personal service. After all, we are serving one another, not performing for the applause of others. We stand before an audience of one!

In Romans 12 and 1 Corinthians 12, the discussion of God-given gifts emphasizes humility and selfless love. Ephesians 4 makes the same point about interdependence and service, but the topic is leadership. Think of the conductor of the symphony. The key to unity amidst such striking diversity is the leader who coordinates the ministries of the body. This unity can only happen when the body members acknowledge that the Lord who has given leaders the gifts is the one who's provided for his church. Leaders, in turn, must acknowledge that they have been placed by "grace." That affects how they see themselves and how they lead. Likewise, as Paul will go on to say, these graced leaders do not serve themselves. They are not the center of attention. Their task is to help all the parts of the symphony come together into a unified whole. Paul now explains how that happens.

Christ became the gift giver by virtue of his victory over sin and death in his ministry on earth. He has shared his bounty with his people. After all, he didn't enter the conflict for his own benefit. Likewise, the results of his victory are not limited just to some future blessings. Christ has bestowed blessings on the church now—on this side of the tapestry.

His gifts to his followers include four types of leaders—apostles, prophets, evangelists, and pastor-teachers. Defining these, particularly in terms that folk in the contemporary church can wrap their heads around, proves a bit confusing at best. Our modern uses of these terms may or may not parallel what Paul is talking about. Overlaying the discussion with our concepts of office, position, and organizational structure just muddies the water.

Nonetheless, we can discover some important principles embedded in these verses.

In light of Paul's previous use of the terms in Ephesians, we can probably confine apostles and prophets to the first-century foundational gifts (Eph 2:19-20). Apostles and prophets received direction from the Lord in unique and special ways that kept the church anchored to the gospel message about Jesus. "He gave some to be" clearly indicates that these terms didn't apply to everyone.

If apostles and prophets were foundational, possibly evangelists formed the extensional arm of the church. These were proclaimers of the gospel who took the message to new places and people. An evangelist may have had a ministry that focused primarily on outsiders. Later, Paul would challenge Timothy "*do to the work of an evangelist*" (2 Tm 2:4). In this case, Timothy was a "troubleshooter" sent from the outside to help stabilize and strengthen the church at Ephesus. He was an extension of the original church planter's work.

Given the sentence structure of the original language, pastor-teacher appears to be a single "office." In his list, Paul uses a definite article with each of the first three positions (apostles, prophets, and evangelists). With pastors-teachers, he uses a single definite article with the two joined by "and." Pastor or shepherd describes the functional term for this leader, while teacher refers to the primary activity by which the pastor does this ministry. Pastor was the common term for the leadership role of the local congregational leaders. Often such a person was older (elder) hence the use of the familiar Jewish term for a religious leader. Overseer, a parallel term, described the same position in terms of function (caregiver, one who looked after others). All of these various terms are used interchangeably in the New Testament (See Acts 14:23; Acts 20:17-28; 1 Tm 3:1-7; Ti 1:5-9).

Leadership—A Gift of Grace

Paul emphasizes the source of these leadership positions—Christ, the victorious gift-giver. He gives to some, but not all, the responsibility of filling these tasks. Rather than being elites who have risen through the ranks of church life, they are God-chosen servants selected and gifted by the Master to fulfill a needed role. Most important, they are there for the church. The church is not there for them.

The needed character qualities of these leaders are outlined in 1 Timothy 3 and Titus 1. Beyond that, scripture provides little to no information about how such leaders were identified and selected for their positions. The bottom line for Ephesians 4 is the gracious source of such leaders. Such leaders are products of his grace. The Lord ultimately determines the who, when, and where. Recognizing this truth can help keep the church from placing its leaders on idolatrous pedestals or, on the other hand, seeing them as menial functionaries. It can also refrain leaders from morphing into tyrannical dictators who rule rather than serve the church.

Leaders With a Purpose

Paul now turns the spotlight on the function of these leaders and the intended goal of their ministries. He explains how such leaders can know they have successfully completed a job well done. This may not prove to be what we often assume.

The fourfold ministry gifts that *Christ the Victor* gave to his people have one primary purpose—*to prepare God's people for works of service*. The works may be diverse, but the intended outcome is singular—so that the body of Christ may be built up. Leaders are not intended to be self-serving.   They are not performers who do ministry for a crowd of admiring spectators. Certainly, they do not seek to restrict the ministry of others in the body. They don't control ministry. They unleash it.

Our English translations have created a history of confusion about this principle. Consider the King James Version rendering of vss. 11 and 12 —*And he gave some, apostles; and some, prophets; and some, evangelists; and some, pastors and teachers; For the perfecting of the saints, for the work of the ministry, for the edifying of the body of Christ....*" Now compare the New International Version, "*It was he who gave some to be apostles, some to be prophets, some to be evangelists, and some to be pastors and teachers, to prepare God's people for works of service, so that the body of Christ may be built up....*"

The punctuation of Verse 12 deserves special attention. The KJV places a comma after the word "saints." The NIV doesn't. The NIV renders the same Greek term for *saints* as "God's people." Punctuated as in the KJV, church leaders have three jobs: 1) the perfecting of the saints, 2) the work of ministry, and 3) the edifying of the body of Christ. Punctuated as in the NIV: church leaders are to do one thing for one reason—prepare God's people for ministry to strengthen the church.

But the context (4:7, 16) and the Greek syntax (there is a change of prepositions after the first "for") suggest that the task of those with these leadership gifts is to equip (NASB) the saints so that the saints may do the work of service (or ministry), to the building up of the body of Christ. Of course, evangelists and pastor-teachers are also engaged in the work of the ministry. But the point is—they don't do it by themselves or for themselves. They share ministry and train others for ministry.

The term translated as "prepare" or "equip" meant to get ready. The verbal form of the same term was used to describe James and John mending their fishing nets. In classical Greek, the ancients used the term to describe restoring a dislocated limb or setting broken bones. It was also used for furnishing a spare room in preparation for guests.

Christ gave (graced) the church with leadership ministries for the purpose of teaching and training others so that they would be prepared to serve the Lord in accordance with their individual abilities. Leadership ministry delegates and multiplies ministry. Paul advises Timothy similarly in 2 Timothy 2:2, *"And the things you have heard me say in the presence of many witnesses entrust to reliable people who will also be qualified to teach others."*

The purpose of these works of ministry is to "build up" the body of Christ. Strengthening the church remains the unwavering goal of the equipping ministry of the leaders. That was Paul's last word to elders of the Ephesian church in their farewell meeting, *"Now I commit you to God and to the word of his grace, which can build you up and give you an inheritance among all those who are sanctified"* (Acts 20:32). The word rendered "build up" was used literally for the actual process of building a house. Figuratively, as here, it referred to strengthening and outfitting a group of people for the task at hand. In this same chapter, Paul uses the word to describe the task of individual believers "building up one another in love" (vs. 16) and the power of wholesome words to "building up" those who hear (vs. 29).

What a Healthy Church Looks Like

Christ gives his people the gift of leaders so these leaders can equip the people for ministry, resulting in the upbuilding of the church. Paul insists that when this "building up" happens effectively, three results will develop—unity, intimacy, and maturity. Each provides an important insight into what a healthy church should look like.

—Unity (*"until we all reach unity in the faith"*). This is probably best understood in terms of the *Seven Ones* previously mentioned. These key principles of belief outline the core of Christian teaching. No congregation and its leaders ought to be satisfied until everyone is moved toward a wholehearted understanding and commitment to these basic concepts. Of course, this remains a work in progress. Individual believers may be at different points in their understanding of the faith. We should expect this in a church that regularly welcomes new believers and includes a cross-section of generations. Not everyone will be at the same stage of growth and knowledge at the same time. But the church and its leader must recognize this reality and make plans to do something about it.

When everyone in the symphony plays the same score, the result is a pleasing melody that glorifies the Lord and catches the attention of a watching world. Without unity of the faith, the resulting chaos dishonors Christ and turns away unbelievers.

—Intimacy (*"in the knowledge of the Son of God"*). A built-up believer experiences a growing personal relationship with Christ. This means more than just increasing the knowledge of biblical facts and doctrine. Those matter, but they are not the real goal. The term for knowledge used here describes more than head knowledge. It emphasizes heart knowledge. Such personal intimacy with Christ shows itself in a changed life, a growing desire to know him more, and an increasing ability to live at peace with others.

Peter explains this best. *"His divine power has given us everything we need for life and godliness through our knowledge of him who called us by his own glory and goodness. Through these he has given us his very great and precious promises, so that through them you may participate in the divine nature and escape the corruption in the world caused by evil desires."* He goes on, *"For this very reason, make every effort to add to your faith, goodness; and to goodness, knowledge; and to knowledge, self-control; and to self-control, perseverance; and to perseverance, godliness; and to godliness, brotherly kindness; and to brotherly kindness, love. For if you possess these qualities in increasing measure, they will keep you from being ineffective and unproductive in your knowledge of our Lord Jesus Christ. But if anyone does not have them, he is nearsighted and blind, and has forgotten that he has been cleansed from his past sins"* (2 Pt 1:3-9).

A church's leaders should desire that individual believers develop a personal desire to grow in faith and their relationship with Christ. This will most often be expressed in personal devotional life, increasing prayer, deeper worship, greater generosity, more and more consistent life of moral and ethical decisions, activities of service to those around them, and a zeal for seeing those who don't know Christ come to accept and serve him. Leaders should ask themselves, "How is our congregation doing? What can we do better?"

—Maturity (*attaining to whole measure of the fullness of Christ*). This describes a final piece that ties the whole together. The ultimate measure of a "built-up body" is Christ. Are we living by the teachings of Jesus? Are we following the example of Christ? Are we looking more and more like Jesus in our way of life? We dare not settle for the standard of the world around us or our culture. Just being above average is not enough. Will we ever perfectly reach this goal in this life? Probably not. Thinking we have is probably the first clue that we haven't arrived. But recognizing our imperfections doesn't permit us to lower the standard.

Here lies every congregation's and its leaders' mission—equip people, build up the church, and work toward every believer's unity, intimacy, and maturity. Mission impossible? In our power, probably. But in his power, it remains another matter. Either way, this is the assignment!

Paul now explains why this assignment is so important and what Christian maturity looks like in practice.

The opposite of maturity is childishness. Christ called his followers to be childlike in their innocence and eagerness to please him (Mk 10:13-15). But childlikeness and childishness are not the same thing. A small child can be cute. A forty-year-old that acts like a two-year-old is not.

But Paul raises the stakes even higher. He uses the vocabulary of infancy, not just childhood. The word he uses describes little infants that can't even speak or feed themselves. An infant is totally dependent. Paul does not elaborate on the word picture, but he could have. A baby human may be cute but is usually helpless. They can't walk. They must be carried about by the will and the whim of someone else. They can seldom tell you what they want. Others must care for their every need. No one expects much from them. That may be expected and acceptable in a tiny infant but not in a Christian believer. Such behavior has serious consequences. A failure to move toward maturity will inevitably affect the unity and vitality of the whole body.

A consequence of spiritual immaturity is instability. Paul likens it to a small boat adrift on the ocean, tossed back and forth by waves and wind. The wind changes. The boat moves with it. The wind changes again, and the boat heads in a new direction. An immature believer often has no fixed convictions. One day they think one way; the next day, another. They are easily moved by whatever seems to be the conventional wisdom of the day.

Instability is one problem. Vulnerability is another. Immature believers seldom prove a match for the many spiritual predators that abound. Paul refers to doctrines promoted by unscrupulous teachers who use "trickery" to fool would-be victims. "Trickery" comes from the Greek term from which English gets the word cube or dice. Literally, it referred to wicked dice playing and figuratively to intentional fraud or sleight of hand. Dice were often "loaded" so the dishonest gambler could manipulate the outcome. Similarly, these false teachers would manipulate scripture to create whatever outcome they desired. They could easily fool a gullible believer.

Paul now outlines this "bodybuilding" process. Mature, stable believers result from leaders who speak the truth in love. Such leaders don't try to offend others, but they will if they must. Truth and love provide a powerful vaccination against vulnerable immaturity. Leaders work toward church growth. But the desired growth is not just numbers. They want their people to grow up, to be able to feed themselves, and stand on their own two feet. And again, the standard is Christ—his teachings, his example, and his mission. When believers are in line with that standard, leaders can rest assured they are on their way to maturity.

Christ remains the head—the defining and controlling agent of the body. Leaders must submit to that truth. They must work to see that those who follow them also share that standard. Our unity stands or falls on our relationship and submission to Christ. If we all fix our eyes on him and commit ourselves to growing closer and closer to him, we will, by definition, experience greater and greater unity. That's a fact!

Such unity grows from the whole body working together. It takes only one weak link to break the chain. That explains why equipping and building up the whole body must be the goal. No one left behind. Every part is needed. We are stronger together. Apart we are partial, incomplete, and vulnerable. Unity matters.

Effective leaders and a unified fellowship of believers always yield a healthy, growing church. Paul now turns to his definition of what Christian maturity looks like in the lives of committed Christians. He has outlined the goal. He next describes the particulars.

Chapter Eight: Swimming

Upstream

So I tell you this, and insist on it in the Lord, that you must no longer live as the Gentiles do, in the futility of their thinking. They are darkened in their understanding and separated from the life of God because of the ignorance that is in them due to the hardening of their hearts. Having lost all sensitivity, they have given themselves over to sensuality so as to indulge in every kind of impurity, and they are full of greed.

That, however, is not the way of life you learned when you heard about Christ and were taught in him in accordance with the truth that is in Jesus. You were taught, with regard to your former way of life, to put off your old self, which is being corrupted by its deceitful desires; to be made new in the attitude of your minds; and to put on the new self, created to be like God in true righteousness and holiness.

Therefore each of you must put off falsehood and speak truthfully to your neighbor, for we are all members of one body. "In your anger do not sin": Do not let the sun go down while you are still angry, and do not give the devil a foothold. Anyone who has been stealing must steal no longer, but must work, doing something useful with their own hands, that they may have something to share with those in need.

Do not let any unwholesome talk come out of your mouths, but only what is helpful for building others up according to their needs, that it may benefit those who listen. And do not grieve the Holy Spirit of God, with whom you were sealed for the day of redemption. Get rid of all bitterness, rage and anger, brawling and slander, along with every form of malice. Be kind and compassionate to one another, forgiving each other, just as in Christ God forgave you.

Ephesians 4:17-32

At the start of Chapter 4, Paul calls these young Christians to live out a new understanding of reality. "Live a life worthy of your calling," he challenges them. If one of God's primary purposes for them is unity, and it is, then followers of Jesus need to take the necessary steps to demonstrate that unity in their church and their lives. That calls for a Christlike attitude and conduct. It also requires leaders who can help individual believers learn to work together and grow together into more and more Christlike lives. Now, Paul begins to explain what such lives look like and what they ought not to look like.

A New Way of Life

The passage is divided into three sections. In Verses 17-19, Paul writes concerning the new relationship to the world in which believers live. In Verses 22-24, he examines the Christian's relationship to the flesh, our old nature. In between, in Verses 20-21, the apostle reminds the Ephesians that in coming to faith in Christ, they didn't just have their past sins forgiven; they also began a journey down a path toward a new way of life. From Verse 25,

Paul gets very specific, describing the behaviors Christians must abandon and those which they must totally embrace. When this takes place, the believer is on the road to living a life that is worthy of his/her calling (4:1). This is the Christian measure of maturity (4:13).

The Christian life is, by definition, different. A believer's priorities, perspectives, and lifestyle have changed. The old is gone. The new has come (Gal 5:17; Col 3:1, 10). This new life stands in stark contrast not only to the believer's old life but also to the unbelieving world around him. "Gentiles" refer to the pagan idolatrous population that surrounded the Christian community. Ethnically and culturally, many of the Ephesian believers were born and raised Gentile. Pagan religions tended to be philosophical or amoral. Religion meant learning and embracing certain ideas or following certain prescribed ceremonies. Seldom did it actually affect the day-to-day lifestyles of the participants. For many, religion had nothing to do with sexual behavior or business practices. Religion was all about ideas and rituals.

Paul explains Gentile conduct in strong terms. Bad behavior flowed from bad thinking. He describes their thinking as "futile." The word meant empty or vain, as in the familiar phrase from Ecclesiastes, "vanity, vanity, all is vanity." Their minds were "darkened." They couldn't see what should have been obvious. They were "ignorant" not because they were stupid or uneducated but because their hearts had grown hard and their consciences calloused.

Ultimately, the issue was more spiritual than intellectual. Unbelievers failed to recognize the reality of the unseen or the promises yet unrealized in this life (Heb 11:1). They mistakenly thought that life amounted only to the knots, loose threads, and confusing colors seen from the underside of the tapestry. They didn't know what they didn't know. "Eat, drink, and be merry for tomorrow you die" was the only perspective that made sense.

The Road We Once Walked

Interestingly, Paul ends his indictment of the ancient pagan society with the claim that "having lost all sensitivity, they have given themselves over to sensuality so as to indulge in every kind of impurity, and they are full of greed" (4:18-19). That reads like the TV guide listings for tonight's cable offerings. Some mistakenly suppose this generation has a corner on the perennial vices of money, sex, and power. They are not modern inventions. Long ago, the New Testament termed them *the lust of the flesh, the lust of the eyes, and the pride of life*" (1 John 2:16). Our culture may have perfected the trio, found new ways to express them, and created expanded media to put them on worldwide display, but such sins are nothing new. Paul now points to the alternative.

Paul had likely been involved in the conversion of many of his readers. He knew exactly how they came to faith, the teachings they received, and the example he and other Christian leaders had set. In other words, they had no excuse. They could not plead ignorance. He knew they understood the ethical and moral implications of their faith.

"To put off" pictured changing clothes, taking off a dirty, sweat-soaked shirt after a hard day's work, cleaning up, and putting on something fresh and clean. No one takes a bath and then puts the same old stinky clothes back on. A clean life requires clean clothes. "Being corrupted" presented a graphic image. Corruption was a term used to describe rotting, decaying garbage or even a corpse. That was our old life. Eventually, that lifestyle would have taken us to very dark places. We can be glad we are rid of all that.

These lines from Ephesians also provide important insight into the evangelism process employed by Paul. When he first preached the gospel in Ephesus, he obviously placed a heavy emphasis on teaching. He didn't just outline a few simple truths that promised to take a person to heaven, ask them to say a prayer, point them toward a baptismal site, quickly bless them, and move on. Somebody, Paul or those on his team, taught them about Jesus. They instructed these new believers to follow the teachings of Jesus. They had insisted that repentance meant a change of direction. Conversion meant a new way of living. A new faith called for a new mode of thinking, a fresh lens through which to view the world around them.

Paul will continue in the next section to explain what this looks like. Here, he simply outlines the new life. It is "God-like." The God of heaven sets the standard, not family, friends, or the latest fashion. "But everyone is doing it" no longer works. God-like norms call for righteousness and holiness. Righteousness can sometimes be translated as "justice" or "rightness." Here, it likely refers to a good or "right" life in the horizontal relationships with people. This is the essence of godliness. Holiness speaks to the vertical dimension of faith. Most often, it referred to a singular devotion to God that called for religious, moral, and ethical purity. Anything less defiled a person before the Living God.

Heaven's Blueprint

In this final section of Ephesians 4, Paul paints a vivid picture of the new life in Christ with six different examples. Each explains what it takes to build a strong, unified Christian fellowship. Take away any of these and unity evaporates. With each specific illustration, he offers a positive and negative alternative to proper Christlike conduct and couples the challenge with a reason or motivation. This is the blueprint God uses as he works in our lives.

Example 1: Like shedding dirty clothes, the godly person must take off the habit of deceitful talk. Lying springs from a desire to either hurt someone else or protect ourselves. Pride or fear almost always lurks nearby. Before coming to faith in Christ, we may have not given much thought to our words. We said whatever made us look good. But that has changed.

Paul probably had Zechariah 8:16 in mind. "*Speak the truth to one another.*" This provided a positive alternative. He adds the motivation, "For we are members of one another." No longer is it enough to simply think of ourselves. We are part of something bigger. Here lies our strength and unity.

Example 2: Anger always corrupts. Everyone gets angry. That's not the problem. To a degree, anger is an emotion. One could even make the case that anger is necessary. A person who is never angry never cares. The problem develops when the emotion becomes words or actions. "*In your anger, do not sin.*" James reminds us that the anger of man does not produce the righteousness of God (1:20).

The positive alternative is to "*not let the sun go down while you are still angry.*" Anger, like steam in a boiler, eventually explodes unless the pressure is released. The longer anger simmers, the greater the danger. Apologizing, clarifying, or in some way resolving the issue today prevents a bigger problem tomorrow. Why does this matter? Unresolved anger leaves the door open for the Devil. He gains a foothold, a point of leverage in our lives. Unresolved anger never remains personal. It has spiritual consequences. Anger is a Trojan Horse. Allowed entry into our lives, it becomes the means of our destruction.

"*A foothold for the devil*" provides a vivid image. Literally, the word referred to a "toehold." A skilled mountain climber can make his way across ice fields and up sheer granite walls if he can find even a small toehold. He doesn't need a bulldozer to clear a road to the top. Just a toehold! Likewise, Satan doesn't require a four-lane highway to create havoc in our lives. A toehold will do just fine!

Example 3: New life in Christ turns a taker into a giver. Theft has no place in a godly life. The positive alternative is not going without, but going to work. But even laboring by the sweat of one's brow and providing for oneself is not the goal. Christ-followers don't just work to eat. They work to share with those in need.

"Doing something useful with their hands" elevated common labor to a place of honor. The ancients often celebrated the life of leisure and considered manual labor undignified. Some moderns haven't progressed too far beyond that mindset. Brother Lawrence, in the classic *Practicing the Presence of God,* caught the spirit of Christ when he learned that any job, no matter how menial, could become a "sacrament" if done to glorify God. As Paul wrote in Colossians, *"And whatever you do, whether in word or deed, do it all in the name of the Lord Jesus, giving thanks to God the Father through him"* (3:17).

Example 4: Paul turns to the power of words again—"No more unwholesome talk." What we say matters. *Unwholesome* pictures something that is rotten or decaying. Literally, it might refer to a dead fish left on the bank or a piece of fruit turning dark and inedible. Here, it describes talk that is harmful and destructive. It is not just that the words are inappropriate. It is more than that. This, of course, includes coarse, off-color talk. But it probably refers more to bitter, critical, and sarcastic conversations.

The believer replaces such useless conversation with words that build up. Imagine what would happen if everything that came out of our mouths contributed something positive to the hearer. What a different world we would live in! Imagine a church without gossip, backbiting, senseless criticism, and general unkindness. Paul takes it a step further. Our words should give grace to those who hear.

Example 5: The last two exhortations tie it all together. *"Do not grieve the Holy Spirit."* The believer's life has become a dwelling place of the Living God. He has taken up residence through his invisible but very real and powerful Spirit to guide and empower us from the inside out. Grieving the Spirit describes a heart of disobedience and rebellion. The expression may have been an illusion to Isaiah 63:10, *"Yet they rebelled and grieved his Holy Spirit."* Wanting to please God rather than disappoint him must become the controlling issue of the Christian walk. That is ultimately why we do what we do.

Example 6: Finally, Paul outlines six specific behaviors that destroy Christian fellowship, undermine our spiritual life, and grieve the Savior who loves us deeply. All six are both relational and personal. Each grows from within and bears its destructive fruit in those closest to us. Ultimately, our words reveal the deadly seeds that are secretly sprouting on the inside.

Bitterness refers to a spirit of resentment. It refuses all attempts at reconciliation. Bitterness easily grows into wrath—a subtle, persistent attitude of antagonism toward someone else. Wrath may be the slow simmer on the inside. Anger happens when what is on the inside explodes. It becomes a temper tantrum. Brawling, a seldom used word, describes the words that often come out during fits of anger. Angry verbal outbursts can be loud and are seldom helpful. Regret almost always follows.

Slander is the word sometimes translated as "blasphemy." Here, it carries a less religious connotation and describes words that target another person. The words are hurtful, abusive, and intended to cause pain and injury. Such talk has no place in the mouth or life of a godly person. All of these behaviors spring from the next word—malice. Malice is a general term for wickedness and evil. Nothing good happens where malice reigns.

The positive alternatives could not be more striking. In a sense, Paul is saying that a person doesn't need to worry about the six bad behaviors. Anyone who concentrates on their opposites will have little room for undesirable problems. Where kindness, compassion, and forgiveness grow, bitterness, wrath, anger, brawling, slander, and malice don't have a chance. The reason for majoring in these positive alternatives—that's how Christ has treated us. This last verse deserves a closer look.

Listening to the Right Angel

This last verse (32) may be one of the hardest verses in the Bible. It may not look like it on the surface, but dig a bit deeper and you may be tempted to quickly move on to something a bit more comfortable and less convicting. This verse almost always creates two simultaneous and contradictory responses in us. If we were in a cartoon strip, this is where an angel would sit on one shoulder and a little devil on the other. Both would be whispering in our ears.

The good angel would draw us to this verse. It would point out how appealing the words are. The good angel will make us yearn to experience its truth. Our heart would cry out, "I need that; I want that. I want to be like that." On the other hand, the devil on our other shoulders will tell us this verse is nothing but nonsense. He will say, "Someone is just trying to make you feel guilty. Don't fall for it." Or that darker voice will whisper, "This is exactly what that person sitting over there needs to hear. Thank God, you don't have that problem."

Listen to one and you will find yourself on the path to joy, contentment, and goodwill. Listen to the other, and you will discover a bitter, painful, and even pitiful life that will only worsen with time. You may argue that your misery is somebody else's fault. But if the truth be told, your plight flows from the decision to listen to the wrong voice.

Look closely at that last verse: "*Be kind and compassionate to one another, forgiving each other, just as in Christ God forgave you.*"

The single sentence contains four key ideas—all connected. First, it offers two imperatives, or commands—*be kind and compassionate to one another.* Secondly, it notes a real-life example of something that always accompanies true kindness and compassion—*forgiving each other.* The sentence ends by explaining why forgiving is not optional for the follower of Jesus—*just as in Christ God forgave you.*

"Kind" is the same term used in the list of the fruits of the Spirit. *"The fruit of the Spirit is love, joy, peace, patience, kindness, and goodness"* (Galatians 5:22). The ancients used the word to describe a wine that had become mellow with age as opposed to wine that had gone bad and turned sour and bitter. When referring to people, it described a person who was good-hearted, friendly, and pleasant to be around as opposed to someone who was hard, harsh or bitter. We all have known both kinds of people. In fact, I would wager we all could name both kinds right now. It is a fact—life has different effects on different folk. The years turn some better and some bitter. The appeal of the text—be kind.

For the ancients, the second imperative—*be compassionate*—was literally a medical term that meant a healthy bowel. But over time, the term became a figurative expression to describe a deep, inner sense of sincere mercy. We do similar things when we speak of a "gut feeling" or nervousness as "butterflies in our stomach." When we speak of compassion, we usually refer to the heart, not the bowel. Hence, older translations render the phrase "be tenderhearted." The emphasis is on a benevolent attitude and then on actions that are totally sincere. This is mercy that is not just superficial.

What does a kind and compassionate person look like? Kindness is most often evidenced in how we talk to and about other people. Some folks are known for their bitter words, others for sweetness. Tenderheartedness, or compassion, is how we are to treat people or react to them when they are less than nice to us. Note these are positive commands. They are not neutral. It doesn't say ignore them, or keep your distance, or be sure you don't retaliate when someone irritates you. Be kind and compassionate to one another!

Be kind and compassionate—that's the two imperatives of the verse. The third part of the verse takes kindness and compassion a step further—*forgiving one another.* Forgiveness is the ultimate test of our character and faith. Kindness and compassion may be easy toward those who are kind and compassionate to us. It is another matter to be kind and compassionate to those who need our forgiveness!

Dumping Our Rock Collection

The fourth part of the verse explains why—*just as in Christ God forgave you.* We extend forgiveness not because it is easy. It isn't. We don't forgive because it is the natural human response to the fact that we run into nasty people in life. There is nothing natural about forgiveness. Revenge is natural. Anger, bitterness and retaliation are the normal responses when we have been wronged. That's why we can't look anywhere other than Jesus for our example. That's why Christians must be forgivers. We are forgiven!

Everyone knows how hard it is to forgive. We have all been wronged at some time in some way by someone. Some of us carry some horribly deep scars. We have been wounded and hurt in ways that we will never forget.

Perhaps it happened when you were young. A classmate bullied you. A older sibling mistreated you. Maybe even a parent or other relative abused you. You've never forgotten, and, more importantly, you have never forgiven.

It could have happened at work. A boss unfairly fired you or passed you over for a promotion. A co-worker could have lied about you, blamed you for something they had done wrong, or claimed credit for something you worked hard to accomplish. Maybe the company for which you had worked hard and faithfully short-changed you or dumped you like just another worn-out piece of machinery. You have never gotten over something that happened twenty years ago. Like a splinter just below the surface, it festers.

And, of course, the hurt could have happened at a place where precious memories should have been created. A marriage could have ended in divorce. Angry words were said. Feelings were hurt. Scars were inflicted that have never healed. Maybe they never will.

As bad as all of that is—I also know there's something else that can hurt just as bad and possibly worse. Sometimes, people get hurt at church. I am absolutely certain of that. I know because I have seen it. I know how mean, low-down, and rotten church folk can sometimes get. Maybe it has something to do with the varnish used on church pews. Perhaps it is toxic when it rubs off and gets in our blood. If only it were that simple! But even if I didn't know this truth by experience, I would know from the words in this verse, *to one another*! This is written to Christians. We're talking church stuff here!

Kindness, compassion, and forgiveness matter to the Lord. His reputation is at stake, too. Christians who don't act like Christians rob his glory and give non-believers good excuses to dismiss and ignore him. If these matters weren't important, they wouldn't play such a prominent role in scripture. This is not just good advice. Kindness, compassion, and forgiveness are true marks of godliness.

Let me change the word pictures. Every time we are hurt, criticized or treated unfairly in life, it is like we have been hit with a pebble or small stone someone has thrown at us. Sometimes, it hits us just right and hurts—a lot. Other times, it is just a passing annoyance. Either way, we must decide what to do. We can go on or we can stop, pick up the stone, put it in our pocket, and take it with us. Who knows, we might get a chance to throw the rock back someday! If we are not careful, as the years pass, we can gather quite a rock collection. The more we carry, the heavier our load, the slower our pace, and the less room we have to gather the better things in life.

Actually, Paul isn't finished with this discussion. He continues the train of thought beyond the chapter division. The following verses provide a fitting exclamation point to the exhortations of this section.

✝

Chapter Nine: Our New Motivation

Follow God's example, therefore, as dearly loved children and walk in the way of love, just as Christ loved us and gave himself up for us as a fragrant offering and sacrifice to God. But among you there must not be even a hint of sexual immorality, or of any kind of impurity, or of greed, because these are improper for God's holy people. Nor should there be obscenity, foolish talk or coarse joking, which are out of place, but rather thanksgiving. For of this you can be sure: No immoral, impure or greedy person—such a person is an idolater—has any inheritance in the kingdom of Christ and of God.

Ephesians 5:1-5

Chapter 5 continues Paul's appeal to live a life reflecting the reality of Christ's actions in our lives. No longer do we look outward, to our culture and surroundings, for the priorities of life. Nor do we look inward as if our self-centered inclinations can provide the needed insights for a "good life." We can't look back to what we have always been taught or what we or "our people" have always done. Our only option is to look up with fresh eyes to what God is doing. Since God is at work, then he and he alone can be our guide and model for life.

From Theory to Life

Ephesians 4 is a turning point in the letter. The first three chapters provide the foundation upon which the last three stand. The former provides the principles; the latter the practice of those principles. Some call this pivot belief/behavior or doctrine/duty. "Then" or "therefore" signals the transition. Believers are challenged to "live a life worthy of the calling." Throughout the rest of the letter, Paul outlines what that life, or walk, should and shouldn't look like. The call is both personal and corporate. Some of the issues he calls attention to very much fall under "personal ethics." Others involve the corporate relationships within the church and family. But even the "personal" matters spill over into the fellowship of the church. Nothing a believer does is a purely private matter.

A worthy life leaves no room for bitter, angry, and fractured relationships. The fruit of unity cannot survive where such divisive weeds thrive. The opening lines of Chapter 5 tie all of the previous obligations together under a single banner—love. Just love one another and everything else will take care of itself. That is exactly how he explains it in Colossians, *"And over all these virtues put on love, which binds them all together in perfect unity"* (3:14). Here in Ephesians 5, Paul will make this appeal from a slightly different direction.

Paul offers a final word on the Christian life in these first two verses of Chapter 5. "Follow God's example!" That's the standard for Christian conduct. The keyword translated "follow" here is the English term from which we derive the word "mimic." It is the act of imitation. We watch what someone does and try to do the same. That's how we learn most things, including how to live right. We hear the instructions. We also see the model. In another place, Paul would say, *"Follow my example, as I follow the example of Christ"* (1 Cor 11:1). Earlier in Ephesians 5, Paul referred to the Christian's new self "*created to be like God in true righteousness and holiness*" (4:24). Perhaps, John said it the clearest, "*Whoever claims to live in him must live as Jesus did*" (1 Jn 2:6).

Peter offered the identical challenge in a different context. Christ suffered hardship and persecution. So will we. Christ endured with dignity and faith. So should we. "*To this you were called, because Christ suffered for you, leaving you an example, that you should follow in his steps*" (1 Pt 2:21). Peter chooses a different Greek word for "example" from what Paul does in Ephesians 5. Peter's term (literally "to write under") pictured a child learning to write by tracing the outline of letters made by a teacher. That's how kids learn, by watching and trying to match the actions of an adult. Like father like son! We have all witnessed a small boy following his dad in the snow, trying to step into the larger footprints.

Paul identifies three reasons why a believer ought to mimic the example of God displayed in the life of Christ. First, we are children of God. It is in our "DNA" to walk a godly life. Secondly, we are not just children but "beloved" children. We are special in his sight. He has poured out on us "the riches of his grace" (1:7). Grace calls us to follow Christ. Finally, Christ loved us and gave himself for us. His atoning sacrifice demonstrates the full measure of his love for us. That sacrifice became a pleasing offering presented to God. Refusing to respond to him in loving worship and obedience would be an unthinkable act of ingratitude. We follow the one who saved us through the cross and empowers us through his Spirit.

A life of love for one another provides the ultimate demonstration that we are actually following Jesus. Words alone won't do it. Attention to ritual or even highly valued spiritual practices isn't enough. Even self-sacrifice and religious zeal by themselves prove little (1 Cor 13:1-3). One factor and one factor alone mark a person as a follower of Christ—a life of love. Jesus put it this way, "*By this everyone will know that you are my disciples, if you love one another*" (Jn 13:35). That's the grand purpose of God—to weave together a community of believers that demonstrates to a watching world the love and unity that only Christ can create. "Walk in love, just as Christ also loved you!" That's our assignment!

Walking In His Steps

I have found two classic Christian books that have helped me understand better what it means to imitate Christ's example. Both are worth dusting off and reading afresh.

The Imitation of Christ by Augustinian monk Thomas A'Kempis contains a series of devotionals, all calling for a closer walk with Christ. Thomas (of the town of Kempen) anonymously wrote the Medieval Latin book sometime between 1418 and 1427. It immediately became one of the most popular Christian devotional books of all time. The book emphasizes a life of spiritual devotion and contemplation. The author calls for a devotion to Christ that focuses on meditation, prayer, and especially Holy Communion. Despite its antiquity, or perhaps because of it, *The Imitation of Christ* still offers a powerful call for believers to deepen their spiritual lives by following Christ.

A second book presents the same challenge from a different perspective. In the form of a novel, *In His Steps* tells the stories of men and women who explored the question, "What would it mean to follow the example of Christ in everyday life?"

When author Charles Sheldon became the preacher of Central Congregational Church of Topeka, Kansas, in the 1890s, the church leaders informed him that he was expected to preach two sermons each Sunday, one in the morning and one more on Sunday night. Sheldon preferred that they cancel the Sunday evening service. It was supposed to be primarily a youth service, but hardly anyone came. The church board didn't change its mind, so Sheldon adopted Plan B.

Instead of preaching a typical sermon, Sheldon decided to tell a story. Each Sunday evening, he presented an installment in an ongoing fictional drama. To add interest, he ended each episode with a cliffhanger designed to draw the young people back to find out what happened next. Eventually, a growing throng of young adults crowded the Central Church sanctuary to listen to Sheldon's tale.

By the time he brought the story to a close, the preacher had written thirty-one chapters. In 1896, a popular religious newspaper picked up the narrative and ran it as a weekly series. When *In His Steps: What Would Jesus Do* came out in book form, it swept the country like wildfire. It has sold over fifty million copies, making it the most widely published religious fiction book of all time.

In His Steps tells us what happened after a church service was interrupted by what we today would call a homeless man. The dirty, raggedly dressed man offered a challenge to the upscale congregation. The man ended his appeal by saying, "I heard some people singing at a church prayer meeting the other night "All for Jesus.... I kept wondering as I sat on the steps outside just what they meant by it. It seems to me there's an awful lot of trouble in the world that somehow wouldn't exist if all the people who sing such songs went and lived them out. I suppose I don't understand. But what would Jesus do? Is that what you mean by following His steps?"

The book recounts the stories of the people who decided to take that question seriously. A newspaper editor, an actress, a musician, businessmen, parents, students, and laborers—all wrestled with the challenge of putting their faith in Christ into practice by asking themselves what Jesus would do before they made any decision. Some succeeded. Some didn't. All were changed.

That's the issue Paul puts front and center in the opening of Ephesians 5. What would life look like if Christians loved as Jesus loved?

Leaving the Old Behind

Having summarized the call to a new walk (a transformed life) under the heading of imitating God-like love, Paul emphasizes again the different form this life should take. In the previous chapter, he spoke in general terms. In this chapter, he gets specific. He leaves no doubt about where the line between right and wrong now stands. He could not be any clearer.

Paul identifies four categories of behavior that he insists are out of bounds for God's people—sexual immorality, impurity, greed, and obscene talk. The first two likely overlap and include all the variations of sexual sin generally condemned by respectable society. The last two touch areas are often deemed more acceptable. But that is exactly Paul's point. Christian behavior has nothing to do with what is considered appropriate or inappropriate in the eyes of society. It has everything to do with what God wants to build into our lives. Any behavior that diminishes God's glory, tarnishes a Christian's witness, or threatens the unity of God's family must be rejected.

Such behaviors should not "even be hinted at" in the Christian family. In other words, these should be so obviously off-limits that Christian people wouldn't give them a moment's consideration. Literally, the wording says, "not even named." Who would even think that such actions might be acceptable? They could never be thought proper among people who are uniquely devoted to God's service (holy people).

Many of us like to think that we have progressed beyond the problems with which our forefathers wrestled. The truth is we may have regressed. As in Paul's day, these issues are no longer debated, but for the entirely opposite reason. Ancient Christians didn't talk about these sins because they thought them obviously wrong. We don't talk about them because, in far too many instances, the debate is over. And we didn't win the argument! Such behaviors have become an acceptable practice for most in our society, including many who claim to follow Christ.

These ancient Christians faced the same struggles we face. Paul likely mentions what he does because he knows this is the world from which many of his Ephesians friends came. That was their social circle. Many might have had family and friends they left behind when they became followers of Christ. It hadn't been easy. Some may have still felt the pull of the old life. Paul wanted them to know that if they were serious about Christ, the old ways had to remain in the past. When they came to Christ, they made a choice. God was building something new in them. They were either in or out. No straddling the fence!

You Think It's Bad Here!

Ancient Greek and Roman society was awash in sexual degradation. Few thought sexual acts of any kind were a moral issue. Sex was just a natural biological expression. No harm, no foul. In fact, it was worse than that. Many, if not most, ancient religions celebrated sexual promiscuity. Some viewed the ecstasy of sex as an expression of a deep spirituality. Others practiced religious rituals modeled after the orgies of their most revered "gods." Pagan priests and priestesses were sometimes little more than temple prostitutes. Few Greek men thought about limiting sex to their marriage bed, except for their wives! A wife who embarrassed her husband by being unfaithful could be dealt with in the harshest terms. Most considered any and all male sexual activity a normal part of public life.

But all of that changed when a person came to faith in Christ. Jesus taught a higher code. His people considered sex a gift of God intended for a committed marriage. Among Christians, this was true for both husbands and wives. A revolutionary thought in the ancient world!

Sin Is More Than Sex

But note how Paul's discussion isn't limited to sex. He includes the topic of sex. He recognizes that sex is at the center of so many human failings. But he also added "impurity and greed" to his list of concerns. Impurity is a general term that could certainly refer to anything associated with sexual impropriety. Perhaps it puts the spotlight on those "bridge" behaviors that get as close to the line as possible without actually crossing it. Throughout the Old Testament, uncleanness was anything that deemed a person unfit to come into the presence of a holy God.

Greed or covetousness describes the unquenchable quest for more, most often material wealth. The greedy heart makes for an unsatisfied life. A few verses later, Paul will associate greed with idolatry. A greedy man or woman seeks security and meaning in what they possess. Such a pursuit is like putting a paycheck in a purse with a hole in the bottom (Hg 1:6). Or as my grandpa would say, "Pouring money down a rat hole."

Paul raises the ante significantly when he adds to the list of avoided vices: *"obscenity, foolish talk, or coarse joking."* The first term described any talk that was base, off-color, or shameful. The other two terms probably help define the first. Foolish or silly talk is what our conversations should not sound like. It is the kind of stupid, unthinking, idle speech in which people easily engage. The talk may not be "dirty" but it certainly profits no one and belittles everyone who participates. It is often associated with gossip, seldom innocent and always unnecessary. The term translated as "coarse joking" could be used positively as quick-witted or the ability to turn a phrase that brings an admiring smile to everyone's face. But here, it is clearly negative. The word came to be used for the kind of language that called attention to the speaker at another's expense. Together, these three words describe self-centered and destructive words that offer nothing positive and everything that is corrosive and negative.

Paul's commentary is instructive. Such talk is not "fitting" among God's people. The alternative is "thanksgiving." Earlier he had called for speech that is *helpful for building others up according to their needs, that it may benefit those who listen* (4:29). The key to transformed talk is not just eliminating the bad but replacing "bad words" with "good words." What would happen if we only concentrated on talk that built others up and brought everyone involved to a better place? That would certainly contribute to unity and a more positive atmosphere in every church I've ever known!

Paul's bottom line is clear. Immorality, impurity, and greed have no place among the people of God. We may have been that way once. But everything changed when God interrupted our lives. We heard the gospel of Christ. We believed it. He forgave us. But he didn't stop there. He changed us. His Holy Spirit took up residence in our lives. We are under new ownership. We march to a different drummer. Going back to the way we were is unthinkable!

This entire discussion raises some important, albeit controversial, matters. Why do Christians behave the way they do? What's the motive? As our incentive for right behavior, does Christ offer us a carrot or a stick? Or does the gospel introduce something altogether different?

Carrots, Sticks, or Something Better

The two commonly proposed motives for Christian living—the carrot or the stick—both lead to dead ends. Neither the positive promise nor the negative warning will take us where we need to go. Consider the carrot.

It might be argued that we do what is right so that we will go to heaven. Heaven is the reward for being good. That certainly sounds appealing. The problem comes when we try to distinguish this notion from the idea of earning our way to heaven. The logic is unavoidable. We are good in order to get the carrot. In other words, our goal is to be good enough to gain eternal life. If it weren't for the promise of the reward, why would we bother trying to do what is right?

That is exactly the thinking of most, if not all, of the world's religions. Only the details differ. Islam pictures it the clearest. The second chapter (Surah) of the Quran describes the judgment in terms of a large scale. Picture the old balancing type on which a known weight is placed on one side and a commodity to be measured on the other. On the Last Day, according to Mohammed's vision, our good deeds will be placed on one side of a scale and our bad deeds on the other. Whichever is heavier will determine our fate—Paradise or hell fire. The goal is to maximize the good and, therefore, gain heaven.

That may be the convictions of most people, including many who sit in church on a Sunday morning, but it is not the gospel. The hope this perspective offers is an illusion. It overvalues our good deeds and undervalues our bad deeds. Most of all, it makes nonsense of grace.

The cross, not the scales of justice, has always been the symbol of gospel-believing people. The cross becomes totally unnecessary if anyone can achieve the right relationship with God by accumulating a sufficient amount of good deeds. This is Paul's point in Ephesians 2 when he declares with unmistakable clarity, *"By grace are you saved through faith and not of yourselves"* (2:8). Or again in Titus, *"But when the kindness and love of God our Savior appeared, he saved us, not because of righteous things we had done, but because of his mercy"* (3:4-5). In Galatians, he insisted, *"I do not set aside the grace of God, for if righteousness could be gained through the law, Christ died for nothing!"* (2:21).

This brings up a corollary of the "carrot" theory. The way to heaven, it is suggested, is to obey the rules or, in Old Testament terms, follow the Law. Put aside for a moment the question of which rules and what laws. Consider just the principle involved. A rule-keeping life inevitably leads to a number of wrong-headed practices.

A rule-keeping mentality always leads to a quest for the minimum requirement. What is the least I can do to satisfy the rule? If obeying the rule is the standard, there is no point in doing more. That would be a foolish waste of time and energy. Rule keeping churches spend enormous amounts of time debating where to draw the line between enough and not enough.

Rule-keeping to gain heaven also results in the proliferation of "lawyers." "Lawyers" specialize in finding or creating loopholes and ways to get around the rules without actually breaking them. Loopholes always amount to redefinitions of the terms. "Lawyers" or experts on the rules are necessary to keep track of the changing definitions. This then requires "scorekeepers" to help keep track of progress. All of this is necessary once a person begins looking for the minimum requirement for heaven.

Next, rule-keeping soon leads to competition. We all want to know how we are doing. The clearest measure is to compare ourselves to others. If too many folk are outdoing us, then we are forced to question our own status. That will never do. It is easier to prove them wrong. Our confidence depends on keeping ourselves ahead of others. This plays havoc with any concept of unity and servanthood.

Finally, an emphasis on keeping the rules results in an emphasis on appearances. The only rules that matter are the ones people see. Hence, we wash the outside of the cup. Who cares about the inside? Remember Jesus' harsh critique of the religious leaders of his day (Mt 23:5-28).

Many of us can't imagine life without rule-keeping. If we don't have rules to obey in order to motivate us or measure our goodness, why would anyone go to the trouble of trying to be good? Life would be a free-for-all. It is law or license. That's the common logic. But that is not Paul's appeal. We will consider his alternative in a moment.

But what about the stick—the negative motivation for doing good to avoid punishment? We understand the impulse. For some, it is a huge motivation. But again, the problem remains the same. We immediately begin to ask, "How little do I have to do to avoid the punishment?" If our primary reason for our behavior is a fear of hell, we will only do what we think we must to get by. And no more!

Stick avoidance quickly leads to preoccupation with self-preservation. We can easily become like the old joke about the two hikers running from an angry bear. One suddenly stops running to tie his shoe. The other shouts back, "You will never outrun that bear like that." The first responds, "I don't have to outrun the bear. I just have to outrun you! Carrot-chasing deteriorates into competition for first place. Stick-avoiding results in satisfaction with just not being last—or appearing better than most. Above average will do.

The Ethic of Grace

Paul appeals to a third way—the ethic of grace. It is not that he never speaks of the promise of a reward or the threat of punishment. He does. But they are always in the background. They never take center stage. He never makes either the carrot or the stick the primary appeal. He is looking for believers compelled by something far stronger than fear or dreams of personal gain.

Paul was often misunderstood because of his emphasis on grace and Christ's love. He still is. Carrot-chasers and stick-avoiders have difficulty imagining a life that isn't motivated by one or the other. He responds to both in Romans. *"Why not say—as some slanderously claim that we say—"Let us do evil that good may result"? Their condemnation is just!"* (3:8). He immediately follows with one of the most powerful explanations of the atoning sacrifice of Christ to be found anywhere in the Bible (Rom 3:21-28). Later, he counters the same objection, *"What shall we say, then? Shall we go on sinning so that grace may increase? By no means!"* (6:1-2). He follows this with an explanation of what following Christ really means and what must be in the mind of a believer when she first comes to Christ (6:3-7). Paul insists that Christ followers have always been called to a life of moral excellence that has little to do with either the carrot or the stick.

Paul's discussion now explains the Christian's true motives for living a life of holiness and goodness.

Chapter 10: Inside Out Living

Let no one deceive you with empty words, for because of such things God's wrath comes on those who are disobedient. Therefore do not be partners with them. For you were once darkness, but now you are light in the Lord. Live as children of light (for the fruit of the light consists in all goodness, righteousness and truth) and find out what pleases the Lord. Have nothing to do with the fruitless deeds of darkness, but rather expose them. It is shameful even to mention what the disobedient do in secret. But everything exposed by the light becomes visible—and everything that is illuminated becomes a light. This is why it is said, "Wake up, sleeper, rise from the dead, and Christ will shine on you."

Be very careful, then, how you live—not as unwise but as wise, making the most of every opportunity, because the days are evil. Therefore do not be foolish, but understand what the Lord's will is.

Ephesians 5:6-17

Why should a believer in Jesus commit to a life of "goodness, righteousness, and truth?" (Ephesians 5:9). Paul answers that question on three different levels in Ephesians. All three are interrelated. Each assumes the other two. Paul winds these three strands together into a single thread that flows from one end of Ephesians to the other. I live the way I do not to earn God's favor but because I have already received it. This motive has a name—*grace*! As a reason for holy living, this discussion comes into sharp focus in Ephesians 5.

The first motive for a righteous and holy life is *our identity*—who I am. As a follower of Christ, I am a child of God (5:1). I am part of a holy (read—unique or special) people. That's what Paul means when he begins his letter by addressing his readers as "saints." He chose us to be holy and blameless in his sight (1:4). We once were dead but now are alive (2:1-6). He made us members of his household (2:19). All who have come to faith in Him now form the body of Christ—his representation in the world (4:15-16). His people have become children of light in a dark world (5:8-11). We haven't always been people of the light. But we are now! Christ changed us. Since that's who we are, that's why we live as we do. On and on the examples could go.

My behavior is not determined externally but internally by my identity—who I am. Most of us who have raised teenagers remember sending them out on some unsupervised activity with the admonition, "Remember, you are a Thomas (or a Smith or Jones, or a ___. You fill in the blank)." Such words weren't a threat or a promise. They were a reminder for them to live up to who they are. That's the appeal of Ephesians.

"Live a life worthy of the calling you have received" (4:1). Some activities were off limits simply because they were God's people (5:3). Such behaviors were "improper." Coarse talk was just "out of place" (5:4).

Living by the Spirit

The second related appeal is the *indwelling* presence of the Holy Spirit. Obviously, this motive stands connected to the first. The first focused on *who* I am. This second emphasizes *whose* I am. I am not my own. As Paul wrote to the morally compromised Corinthians, *"Do you not know that your bodies are temples of the Holy Spirit, who is in you, whom you have received from God? You are not your own; you were bought at a price. Therefore honor God with your bodies"* (1 Cor 6:19-20). The Holy Spirit is the ultimate internal motivator of righteous behavior. The Spirit is God at work from the inside. *"For it is God who works in you to will and to act in order to fulfill his good purpose"* (Phil 2:13).

Paul emphasized this early in Ephesians, *"And you were also include in Christ when you heard the message of truth, the gospel of your salvation. When you believed, you were marked in him with a seal, the promised Holy Spirit"* (1:13). He hints at this same inner motivation when he wrote, *"For you are God's workmanship, created in Christ Jesus to do good works, which God prepared in advance for us to do"* (2:10). We are *"dwelling in which God lives by his Spirit"* (2:22). This is the source of our strength (3:16). It is his *"power at work within us"* (3:20). Being *"filled with the Holy Spirit"* remains the ultimate aspiration of anyone desiring to follow Jesus (5:18). Contending with the "sword of the Spirit" and "praying in the Spirit" mark the believer's struggle with evil (6:17, 18).

This internal indwelling of the Spirit of God remains the distinctive mark of the Christian life, not carrots or sticks. The prophets looked forward to that reality long before the coming of Christ. They promised the coming of a new kind of relationship with God. The prophets promised that someday the Lord would initiate a "new covenant," a new way of relating to God (Jer 31:3-34). This promise wasn't for the restricted few. The prophets promised this new reality of the Spirit to all of God's people. This would be the answer to Moses' prayer. In Numbers 11, Joshua, Moses' longtime aid, reported that two unauthorized men were "prophesying" in the camp. Joshua wanted Moses to stop them. Instead, Moses offered this response, *"Are you jealous for my sake? I wish that all the Lord's people were prophets and that the Lord would put his Spirit on them!"* (Nm 11:29).

Centuries later, the Lord promised through the prophet Joel, *"And afterward, I will pour out my Spirit on all people. Your sons and daughters will prophesy, your old men will dream dreams, your young men will see visions. Even on my servants, both men and women, I will pour out my Spirit in those days."* (Jl 2:28-29). "This is that," Peter explained on the day of Pentecost. God has kept his promise as a result of the finished work of Christ (Acts 2:14-33). Jesus had said, "another comforter" (Jn 14:26; 15:26-27; 16:7-15) would come. He came. Jesus did exactly what he said he would do. Peter promised that this reality of the Holy Spirit's presence could be the experience of anyone who trusted in Jesus as the Christ, repented of their past rebellion, and submitted to baptism in Jesus' name (Acts 2:38).

Reflecting God's Goodness

Christian behavior is motivated by who we are and whose we are, by our identity and by the empowering presence of the Holy Spirit in our lives. Paul points to a third factor throughout Ephesians. Again, trying to neatly separate these three is futile. All three are from a single united theme: grace. God has freely blessed us. We are driven to return that blessing, not because we are afraid he will take it away if we don't obey the rules or because we believe obeying the rules is a way to gain more rewards but because we are so *overwhelmed by gratitude* that we can no longer conceive of doing less. Ephesians 1 is saturated with this idea. Paul recounts all that God has done for us. He points to God's eternal plan, our redemption in Christ, the promised future he has in store for us, and the Holy Spirit's presence. Three times, this litany of grace overflows in worship. All of this leads "to the praise of his glorious grace" (1:6). Such blessings call "for the praise of his glory" (1:12). The believer's past, present, and future can lead only to one place—"to the praise of his glory" (1:14).

Recognizing God's grace produces gratitude and prohibits any remnants of self-congratulation (2:8-10). Our lives, individually and corporately as the church, have become temples devoted to our God and Savior (2:20-22). Together as the church, regardless of ethnic background, race, class, or any other human category, we live our lives so that the "manifold wisdom of God might now be made known" (3:10). We live to glorify him.

Our words and lives reflect his grace in grateful worship and a Christ-like walk. More than anything, we want "to please him" (5:10). Our goal is to know and do his will (5:17). How could anyone be satisfied with a useless or out-of-control life once they grasp how much God has done for them (5:15-18)? Thankful worship is the only response that makes sense (5:19-20). We walk in the light as people of light because the light of grace has rid our lives of the darkness in which we once walked (5:6-16). He did that. We want the world to know.

All three of these powerful motivators—our identity, his indwelling, and our determination to live in "praise of his glorious grace"—work from the inside. They propel us to levels of devotion and obedience that no carrot or stick alone could accomplish. We don't want to just get by. Satisfying the minimum requirements never crosses our minds. *For Christ's love compels us, because we are convinced that one died for all, and therefore all died. And he died for all, that those who live should no longer live for themselves but for him who died for them and was raised again*" (2 Cor 5:14-15).

Paul organizes this section around five urgent calls to action. None are optional. This isn't a multiple-choice test where we choose the one or two we like best and ignore the rest. Each has real-life consequences associated with it.

Let no one deceive you. Deception is always a possibility. The world, the flesh and the Devil all work hard to blur our priorities and dull our moral sensibilities. Society pushes us toward the common and the popular. Our own desires and lingering memories from the past threaten to sabotage us at every turn. Satan remains the grand deceiver. He may not be able to destroy us, but that doesn't keep him from trying. His aim is simply to neutralize us.

"*Empty words*" provide the common means of deception. False promises about life lived on the dark side, rationalizations about sin, and distractions that keep us too preoccupied to do right abound at every turn. From a distance, it all looks good. It makes sense. But upon closer examination, there is no "there there!" It is all a mirage.

Words matter, even empty ones. Some words matter eternally. In this case, these words lead to nowhere good. The lost world around us will one day face God's righteous judgment because they have listened to such nonsense. Many of us, indeed all of us, know how that happens. Before Christ found us, we were all among the disobedient. That's in the past. That's where it needs to stay! "Be on guard," Paul insists.

Do not be partakers with them. Forewarned is forearmed! We know better. The last thing we should want to do is drift backwards and join in the shameful things we used to do. Some want to take this as a call to totally refrain from any contact with sinners, to build a wall of purity around our lives and refuse to come out. Clearly, this is contrary to Jesus' call to "let our lights shine," to put our witness "on a lamp stand" and not hide it "under a basket" (Matthew

5:14-16). Eventually, a Christian witness requires association without participation.

"Live as children of light." "Live" is that word "walk" we have seen Paul use so often. It describes a way of life. We used to be one way. Now, we are different. We live the way we do because Christ changed us. We have a new identity. The reality of this new life bears the fruit of goodness, righteousness, and truth. Goodness marks a life that brings benefit to others. It is never "good for nothing." Righteousness values what is right and just. A life of truth aligns with the standards of God's reality. This trio parallels the fuller list of the Spirit's produce from Galatians 5:22-23. These are fruits because what shows up on the outside results from what lives on the inside. The character of Christ grows from us because God is at work in us.

"Have nothing to do with the fruitless deeds of darkness, but rather expose them." Most of us know from experience that constantly pointing out the faults of our wayward friends and family seldom accomplishes anything positive. On the other hand, if we live consistently, exhibiting the goodness, righteousness, and truth that should come naturally, the contrast will become apparent. That's all the exposing that is usually required. Consistency, however, is the challenge. Waffling on our part, one minute participating, the next minute abstaining (whatever the questionable behavior may be), and the friend or family member quickly loses all respect for us. While they lose respect, we lose any opportunity we might have had to influence them for Christ.

The last part of Verse 14 ("*Wake up, sleeper, rise from the dead, and Christ will shine on you.*") appears to contain a quotation, likely based loosely on Isaiah 60:1. Some scholars suggest that it might have been lines from an early Christian baptismal hymn. Perhaps the early believers gathered around the new convert, heard the confession of faith in Jesus, and then sang these words after they witnessed the believer's baptism that followed. If so, the lyrics reinforced that call to a new life portrayed in baptism (Rm 6:4). Perhaps the early practice resembled the tradition of the small rural church where I grew up. After every baptism, the congregation would break out in song. It seldom needed prompting. "Now I belong to Jesus. Jesus belongs to me, not for the years of time alone, but for eternity." Every time I hear those lyrics, I remember my own baptism.

Paul sees the Christian life as a series of contrasts. Life before Christ was one way; after Christ, it is totally different. Earlier, he pictured the change as a dead man coming to life (2:1-7). Here, he compares this transformation to the difference between light and darkness, wisdom and foolishness, and drunkenness (out of control) and being filled with the Spirit (under God's control).

"Be very careful how you live." This imperative transitions to the next discussion. The Christian walk does require careful thought and wisdom. Coming to Christ is both a beginning and an end. It is an end to an old way of life and the beginning of a new life. But it is also the beginning of new and sometimes even greater struggles. Before our conversion, our Adversary had us where he wanted us. After we come to Christ, Satan sees us as still vulnerable. He seeks to undermine us before our roots grow deep. If Jesus faced temptation immediately after his baptism, we shouldn't expect anything less. But young or old, all Christians will face moral and spiritual decisions until they draw their last breath. That's life. That's the kind of world we live in.

Every day brings new challenges. No one is exempt. Depending upon one's perspective, these challenges are obstacles _or_ opportunities. Paul's phrase in Verse 16 is variously rendered as "making the most of your time" (New American Standard Bible), "making the most of every opportunity" (New International Version), "redeeming the time" (King James Version), "make the most of every chance you get" (The Message), or "make the best use of your time" (J. B. Phillips New Testament). "Redeeming" in the KJV and "making the most" in most others translates to a word that describes making a purchase in a market or rescuing something about to be thrown away.

"Opportunity" was a term that emphasized not just the passing of time but a particular occasion or moment. Not all days are the same. We can look back and recognize special moments in our lives that became turning points. We remember a day that affected all that followed. Nothing was ever the same after that day. Sometimes, it was good; sometimes, not so much. Wisdom learns to recognize those occasions sooner rather than later and take advantage of the opportunity. As the saying goes, "A few people make things happen. Others watch things happen. Many sit back and wonder what happened." Better to be the men of Issachar, *who understood the times and knew what Israel should do"* (1 Chr 12:32). Knowing God will make the difference.

Paul is now ready to take us into a deeper understanding of inside-out living, motivated and empowered by the Holy Spirit.

Chapter Eleven: Living Under the Influence

Do not get drunk on wine, which leads to debauchery. Instead, be filled with the Spirit, speaking to one another with psalms, hymns, and songs from the Spirit. Sing and make music from your heart to the Lord, always giving thanks to God the Father for everything, in the name of our Lord Jesus Christ. Submit to one another out of reverence for Christ.

Ephesians 5:18-21

Paul continues the list of imperatives that mark the children of light. "*Do not get drunk with wine, which leads to debauchery*" probably falls under the heading of the "fruitless deeds of darkness" noted above. Proverbs struck the right note, "*Wine is a mocker and beer a brawler whoever is led astray by them is not wise*" (20:1). One might argue the pleasures and benefits that come from a moderate consumption of alcohol. Some do. But surely, no sensible person would try to make a case for drunkenness. That would be "a fool's errand." Drunkenness is a waste—of money, time, and good brain cells. No wonder we sometimes refer to a person who has had too much to drink as "wasted!" Drunkenness leads to all sorts of evil and never to anything good.

This is a comparison of contrast, not similarities. Paul is not suggesting that being "*filled with the Spirit*" resembles the euphoric, sometimes ecstatic, out-of-control experience caused by too much alcohol. Some of the pagan religions common in the Greco-Roman world made that connection. The cults of Bacchus and Delphi, for example, promoted the consumption of alcohol or certain hallucinatory drugs as the means to contact the gods. Adherents interpreted the resulting mind-altering stupor as an encounter with the "spirit world." Paul argues the opposite.

For Paul, drunkenness provides a perfect illustration of everything Almighty God doesn't want to happen in our lives. He could just as easily have said, "Look at the life of that drunk stumbling down the street. Now go and do just the opposite." He contrasts the useless results of a drunken stupor with the transforming power of the Holy Spirit. Here are the alternatives—turn control of your life over to intoxicating spirits or be filled with the Holy Spirit. The contrast couldn't be sharper. One is a waste; the other leads to worship. The drunk often picks a fight and grows loud and abusive; the Spirit-filled followers of Christ seek peace and look for ways to quietly serve others.

This call to be "filled with the Spirit" and the results that follow are worthy of a closer examination. This discussion provides yet another look at the work of God in the life of faith. Let's pursue a few of the common questions that arise from these verses.

The Spirit-Filled Life

First, what does it mean to be filled with the Spirit? The short answer—to be filled with the Spirit means to be filled with God. That's what Paul had prayed for a couple of chapters earlier. Remember that benediction, "Now to him who is able to do immeasurably more...." That's the end of Ephesians 3. The prayer comes just before that, "*I pray that you, being rooted and established in love, may have power, together with all the saints, to grasp how wide and long and high and deep is the love of Christ, and to know this love that surpasses knowledge—that you may be filled to the measure of all the fullness of God*" (3:15-19).

Understanding this phrase "*be filled with the Spirit*" requires that we get a handle on the term *spirit*. The Greek word itself, and its corresponding Hebrew term, could refer to the wind or breath. It also came to be used for God's unseen, life-giving presence. It is first used in Genesis 1:2 where the Spirit or Wind of God moved over the surface of the waters. Often, but not always, the word "holy" was added to help distinguish the Spirit of God from the more general use of the word.

A lot of folks are confused by the Bible's talk about the Father, Son, and Holy Spirit. Make no mistake: Christians only worship one God. But this God has chosen to reveal himself to us as Father, Son, and Holy Spirit. All three are God. This has been his nature throughout all eternity. All are the same God, only viewed from slightly different perspectives. Historically, theologians have defined this as one God in three persons. The term "trinity" provides a shorthand for a much larger and complicated philosophical discussion.

Let it suffice to simply say that the Father emphasizes the power and authority of God. The Son reveals God in human form. The creator visited this planet in the person of Jesus Christ. His "only begotten Son" describes this truth in other words. The Spirit demonstrates the nearness of God. In the Spirit, God reaches into our lives invisibly, yet powerfully and personally. The Spirit of God is not new. But after Jesus came, the Spirit began a new kind of work. On the night before the cross, Jesus told his disciples that something new was about to take place. "*Now I am going to him who sent me, yet none of you asks me, 'Where are you going?' Because I have said these things, you are filled with grief. But I tell you the truth: It is for your good that I am going away. Unless I go away, the Counselor will not come to you; but if I go, I will send him to you*" (Jn 16:5-7). Earlier, Jesus made this startling statement, "*Whoever believes in me, as the Scripture has said, streams of living water will flow from within him.*" In the next verse, John adds this word of explanation, "*By this he meant the Spirit, whom those who believed in him were later to receive. Up to that time the Spirit had not been given, since Jesus had not yet been glorified*" (*Jn 7:38-39*).

God kept that promise. Fifty days after the cross, the Apostles announced, "God raised Jesus to life, made him Lord of all, and poured out the promised Holy Spirit." "*Repent and be baptized, every one of you, in the name of Jesus Christ for the forgiveness of your sins. And you will receive the gift of the Holy Spirit*" (Acts 2:36-38). That long-promised new day had arrived. From that day on, the work of the Spirit of God would be from the inside out in every person who personally received Jesus Christ as the Savior and leader of life.

If the Spirit is the presence of God himself working inside the life of the believer, what does that expression in our text "*be filled* with the Spirit" mean? The surrounding verses explain. It is here that Paul contrasts the filling of the Spirit and drunkenness. Most of us know what a DUI is: a citation for *driving under the influence*. Hopefully, few of us know it from experience. In most states, current law says that .08 blood alcohol will put a driver in a heap of trouble. Why is DUI bad? Because alcohol affects everything you do. Reaction time, behavior, perceptions—everything is altered to some degree when a person is "under the influence."

God's will is that a Jesus-follower be so filled with his presence that they live "*under the influence.*" Being filled with the Spirit does not mean getting more of the Holy Spirit. It describes the Spirit getting more of the believer. When that happens, everything is affected.

The text highlights three results of being filled with the Spirit. Some try to define "Spirit fullness" by emotion, ecstatic speaking, or some other manner of eccentric behavior. That's not what this text describes. Here "being filled with the Spirit" has three observable effects. It influences words, attitudes, and relationships. "*Speak to one another with psalms, hymns and spiritual songs. Sing and make music in your heart to the Lord.*" Negativity, criticism, and fear are replaced with joy, encouragement, and hope. "*Always giving thanks to God the Father for everything, in the name of our Lord Jesus Christ.*" Greed gives way to gratitude. "*Submit to one another out of reverence for Christ.*" Servant-mindedness replaces self-will.

How to Be Filled with the Spirit

To be filled with the Spirit is to experience the fullness of God in our lives. It means to live under the influence of God in every area of our lives. *How does that happen?* That's the other question. Our text offers several hints. Without becoming too technical, we need to note a bit of grammar in these verses.

First, "be filled with the Spirit" is an *imperative or command.* True spirituality will only happen when you want it to happen. The Lord may sometimes surprise us with some unexpected spiritual experience. He may do that when he wants our attention. But for the most part, experiencing the fullness of God in your life is not something that will sneak up on you when you least expect it. The Lord allows you to decide how close you want to be to him. The text says this is God's will. Picture it like this. The Lord says, "I vote that your life be lived totally under my influence." He then says, "How do you vote." It takes two to make it happen. This is a command. We respond to commands by obeying. Be careful about pushing this notion too far until you remember this next factor.

Secondly, "be filled with the Spirit' is a *passive imperative.* It *is* a command. We can ask for it, but we can't make it happen. This is a work of God. We are not self-made people. No amount of religious effort, spiritual discipline, or self-help advice will develop the life God wants and we desire. Only He can do it when we ask.

Third, the phrase in our text is a *second-person plural imperative.* That means that what is described in this passage is not some special relationship or experience reserved for super Christians, a special holy elite, or saints and holy men. This is a description of the normal Christian life. Remember Paul's prayer in Ephesians 3. *"I pray that you…may have power, together with all the saints…that you may be filled to the measure of all the fullness of God."*

The Christian life begins with the Holy Spirit. The Christian life grows and develops as the Holy Spirit works in our lives. It is the fruit of the Spirit growing from the inside that makes our Christian life a joy for us and those who know us. The Lord wants to influence every area of our lives. That's the masterpiece he is seeking to weave into our lives. That's his eternal purpose for each of us.

A fourth grammatical note—this is a *present tense command.* In the language the New Testament was written in, this means "being filled with the Spirit" is an ongoing, not a once-and-for-all experience. It doesn't happen once and then you forget about it. It has to happen over and over again. Why? As one old preacher explained, "We leak!"

None of us are perfect. We are still human beings who face temptation and sometimes stumble and fall. To "be filled with the Spirit" means to repeatedly come back for more. We must repeatedly turn parts of our lives over to the will of God to be lived under the influence of the Spirit.

But sometimes that doesn't happen when it should. We experience a time of "spiritual dryness." We lose some of the joy, effectiveness, and spiritual power we know should be ours. We are running on empty. Most of us know that feeling—spiritually and literally.

The human soul doesn't operate well on empty. Some of us have tried. The solution to an empty soul is to "be filled with the Spirit."

Like my car's gas tank, I can't get my spiritual fill once and then coast for the rest of my life. To live efficiently requires frequently seeking a fresh filling from the Spirit of God. How does it happen? The short answer, "Just ask!" Jesus explained it this way, *"If you then, though you are evil, know how to give good gifts to your children, how much more will your Father in heaven give the Holy Spirit to those who ask him!"* (Lk 11:13).

The Five Marks of the Spirit-filled Life

For Paul, the Spirit-filled life is not just an abstract theory or personal emotions. That life manifests itself in specific, observable behaviors. That's where the discussion now takes us. "Be filled with the Spirit" describes a life under the influence of the Spirit of God. The Spirit operates from the inside of our lives. He becomes more than just external rules and social expectations. But that raises another question that Paul now addresses. What does the "Spirit-filled" life look like? He points in directions that we might not expect.

Again, a bit of grammar helps. The imperative (be filled with the Spirit) is followed by a series of participles (actions) that explain the expected fruit or results of that Spirit-filled life. The words in order are: speaking, singing, making music, giving thanks, and submitting. Each offers important insight into the nature of the work of God that Paul calls *"being filled with the Spirit."*

"Speaking to one another with psalms, hymns, and songs from the Spirit." Like alcohol, the Spirit's presence affects our words, but in a much different way. A drunk slurs his speech, becomes loud and boisterous, and maybe abusive. He often becomes rude and ill-mannered, less and less concerned about those around him. The words of a "Spirit-filled" man or woman move in a totally different

direction. Their voice seeks to inspire and draw others to a closer walk with the Lord.

Paul emphasizes the role of music in the Christian fellowship. Music often accompanies drunkenness as well. But drinking songs are seldom known for their beauty or edifying effects on others. A "Spirit-filled" person seeks lyrics and melodies that stir the soul and draws others nearer to God. Such music is not self-serving. Christian worship ultimately requires a community, a gathering of people. Theoretically, I can worship alone. Certainly, we all should. But, at some point, "Spirit-filled" worship requires "speaking to one another."

Paul's mention of singing at this point clearly underscores the importance of music in the Christian fellowship. Sometimes, we think of singing as directed only upward. The phrase "praise and worship music" has become synonymous with God-ward singing. That's not how Paul sees it.

The exhortation to speak to one another in a song lists three kinds of music—hymns, psalms, and spiritual songs. This is probably not intended to be an exhaustive list of the only kinds of acceptable Christian music. "Hymns" likely referred to music directed to God. In Christian gatherings, even when we praise God, others are listening. The mere act of singing praise together adds an important ingredient of inspiration and edification. "Psalms" technically described music sung to the accompaniment of a musical instrument. The term is derived from the Greek word for striking a string. "Songs from the Spirit" or "spiritual songs" was, likewise, a general term for music. The adjective "spiritual" added the clarification that not every popular song would be appropriate among Christians. Believers speak to one another in music inspired by the Spirit or at least songs consistent with the work of the Spirit.

Music Is More Than Entertainment

"Sing and make music from your heart to the Lord." These second and third actions that flow from a "Spirit-filled" life go together. It seems clear that these two overlap with the first. All three involve music. Paul doubles down on this idea because he wants his readers to understand how vital music is to the Christian experience. Far from being the entertainment before the main event, the music is the heart of Christian worship and fellowship. This was true for Hebrew worship in the Old Testament, as evidenced by the large number of Psalms included in scripture and the emphasis placed on singing and musical instruments in the temple services (1 Chronicles 25; 2 Chronicles 5:11-14).

The worship the Spirit inspires flows from the heart. It can't be superficial or merely an act performed for an audience. Soren Kierkegaard, the 19th-century Danish philosopher, struck the right note when he insisted that much of Christendom has worship backwards[3]. We too often, he wrote, view the people in the pews as the audience and the musicians and speakers on the stage as the performers. The performers present their program for the pleasure and approval of the audience in the pews. No, Kierkegaard protested, the people in the pews are the performers. Those on the stage are the conductors who direct the music and the prompters who help the performers remember their lines at the right time. The audience is God. Everyone performs for his pleasure. His approval matters above all else.

"Always giving thanks to God the Father for everything, in the name of our Lord Jesus Christ." Thanksgiving is more than a national holiday. It is bigger even than a worship service. An attitude of gratitude evidences a "Spirit-filled" life. Such a life recognizes that our God is the "giver of every good and perfect gift" (Jm 1:17). Thanksgiving radiates from the music we sing when we are together because it is so much a part of our lives when we are apart. It saturates our conversations as we walk and talk in between. We give thanks in everything because we know that even in the hardest of times, the Father above remains at work, weaving his eternal plan into the masterpiece of our life. A Spirit-controlled life projects gratitude and rejects grumbling. Jesus Christ makes that possible. We know it, and we show it!

The Toughest Assignment of All

"Submit to one another out of reverence for Christ." Paul turns to a fifth action that provides the ultimate test of the Spirit's work. Few would consider encouraging one another through music too difficult a task. Most of us find singing to the Lord enjoyable, perhaps depending on our preferred style of music. Sad but true! We understand the appropriateness of giving thanks. But "submitting to one another"—that's another matter.

Our society has taught us from day one to look out for number one. Our cultural gurus insist that self-care should be our highest priority. Love yourself, think of yourself, and put yourself first, we are told. Then Paul says, "Be filled with the Spirit...submitting to one another." In fact, he considers this so important that he follows with six case studies of what this means in the everyday life of a believer. Some of us might be more comfortable if he had just stopped at the principle and left the application to our own imaginations. We would probably have left ourselves more wiggle room than what the apostle does.

The term "submit" or "be subject to" came from the military world. It referred to ranking behind someone or standing in a line with someone else at the front. If I am the one who submits, I am not the person in charge. I am not the leader. I don't call the shots. I serve at the pleasure of the one to whom I submit. I acknowledge that the one to whom I submit is more important than I am. I consider their wants before I consider my own. The opposite of "submitting" would be to dominate, to demand, or to seek to use others for my benefit. "Submitting to one another" rules out coercion and manipulation. That's a high standard. Most of us find it a difficult task. Maybe that's because only the Holy Spirit can cause it to happen.

"To one another"—Paul makes this an open-ended expectation. Submission to one another is a general Christian standard. It applies equally to all who name Christ as Lord. Recognizing this must start before we begin to tackle the illustrations that follow. This isn't about marriage or parenting, or slave-master relationships. This has priority over any of those social roles. It applies to those roles. But we dare not limit it to these six specific situations.

This is not a new principle. Jesus taught it to his overly ambitious disciples. "*Jesus called them together and said, "You know that the rulers of the Gentiles lord it over them, and their high officials exercise authority over them. Not so with you. Instead, whoever wants to become great among you must be your servant, and whoever wants to be first must be your slave—just as the Son of Man did not come to be served, but to serve, and to give his life as a ransom for many"* (Matthew 20:25-28). Paul insisted on the same truth, *"Do nothing out of selfish ambition or vain conceit. Rather, in humility value others above yourselves, not looking to your own interests but each of you to the interests of the others"* (Philippians 2:3-4).   Whatever you choose to call it, this is "submitting to one another."

Our Motive: Reverence for Christ

Motives matter. Paul says the "Spirit-filled" believer does this "out of reverence for Christ." The Greek word rendered "reverence" is the word normally translated as "fear." In other words, we submit to another person not because the other person deserves it or we fear the punishment the other person will send our way if we don't submit. We do it because of who we are and because of whose we are. Remember the carrots and sticks discussion earlier and the role of our identity in Christ.

We behave a certain way because of our relationship with our Lord. After all, we are talking about a life under the influence of the Holy Spirit! But how does *fear* figure into this? Does a Christian fear God or not? Certainly, the Old Testament taught that the *"fear of the Lord is the beginning of wisdom"* (Prv 9:10).   Ecclesiastes concluded, *"Fear God and keep his commandments, for this is the duty of all mankind"* (12:13). The New Testament teaches much the same principle. Yet the New Testament also insists that *"perfect loves casts out fear"* (1 Jn 4:18). In another place, Paul himself announced that when the Holy Spirit comes into our lives, he transforms our relationship with God from that of a slave to that of a child so that we no longer need to live in fear (Rm 8:15). How do we reconcile these two ideas?

The Two Sides of Fear

Any disharmony evaporates when we recognize two different definitions of fear at work. The two are related, but totally different. Perhaps they are like two sides of the same coin. The great divide between the two definitions happened at the cross and our baptism. The cross demonstrated God's amazing grace and goodness. He was for us, not against us (Rm 8:32). At our baptism (conversion experience), we finally acknowledged that and accepted it as our own. We opened our lives to the work God had wanted us to do all the time. The "fear of God" came out of the shadows and into the light of his love. I may still fear him. I know my place. I recognize his. I don't confuse the two. But I also understand our relationship based on what Christ did on the cross. I am now his child. That changes everything!

✝

Chapter Twelve: Our Most Difficult Assignment

Wives, submit yourselves to your own husbands as you do to the Lord. For the husband is the head of the wife as Christ is the head of the church, his body, of which he is the Savior. Now as the church submits to Christ, so also wives should submit to their husbands in everything.

Husbands, love your wives, just as Christ loved the church and gave himself up for her to make her holy, cleansing her by the washing with water through the word, and to present her to himself as a radiant church, without stain or wrinkle or any other blemish, but holy and blameless. In this same way, husbands ought to love their wives as their own bodies. He who loves his wife loves himself. After all, no one ever hated their own body, but they feed and care for their body, just as Christ does the church—for we are members of his body. "For this reason a man will leave his father and mother and be united to his wife, and the two will become one flesh." This is a profound mystery—but I am talking about Christ and the church. However, each one of you

*also must love his wife as he loves himself, and the wife
must respect her husband.*

*Children, obey your parents in the Lord, for this is
right. "Honor your father and mother"—which is the
first commandment with a promise—"so that it may go
well with you and that you may enjoy long life on the
earth." Fathers, do not exasperate your children;
instead, bring them up in the training and instruction
of the Lord.*

*Slaves, obey your earthly masters with respect and fear,
and with sincerity of heart, just as you would obey
Christ. Obey them not only to win their favor when their
eye is on you, but as slaves of Christ, doing the will of
God from your heart. Serve wholeheartedly, as if you
were serving the Lord, not people, because you know
that the Lord will reward each one for whatever good
they do, whether they are slave or free. And masters,
treat your slaves in the same way. Do not threaten them,
since you know that he who is both their Master and
yours is in heaven, and there is no favoritism with him.*

Ephesians 5:22-6:9

According to an old story, an admirer once asked conductor and composer Leonard Bernstein what was the hardest instrument to play. His answer: "Second fiddle." He explained, "I can always get plenty of first violinists, but to find one who plays second violin with as much enthusiasm, or second French horn or second flute, now that's a problem."

Paul insists that playing "second fiddle," voluntarily putting another ahead of ourselves, is a mark of a Spirit-influenced life. He calls it "submitting to one another out of reverence for Christ" (Ephesians 5:21). For most of us, this call to submission often proves the toughest assignment we will ever face in life.

Paul knows the difficulty most of us will have with this, so he explains what "submitting to one another" should look like in the life of a Christian. He offers six case studies or examples. He might have cited others. For example, he doesn't address the Christian's responsibility to the government. He will in other places (Romans 13:1-7; 1 Timothy 2:1-7). What he highlights touches on the common experiences most believers face in daily life.

Serving Christ by Serving Others

The situations Paul includes in his six case studies mirror discussions found elsewhere in the New Testament and even in the popular writings of the cultural commentators of the Greco-Roman world. Historians refer to this type of material as "household codes." The codes cover the expected conduct of people in their various domestic roles. Other New Testament examples include—Colossians 3; 1 Timothy 2 and 5; 1 Peter 2 and 3; and Titus 2.

It is important to note that Paul provides six case studies, not just three. This is where he departs from the social standards of his day. The non-Christian experts had much to say about the appropriate behavior of wives, children, and slaves. They said next to nothing about the "superior" partner's proper conduct. The dominant culture of Paul's day was largely patriarchal. Men ruled the world. Fathers controlled the family. Males lived by one set of ethical and moral standards, their wives by another much stricter code. Likewise, children had little value in the Greco-Roman world. Obviously, most Greek and Roman parents loved and cared for their children. But the expectations were low. Physical abuse was common. Families wanted a male heir to carry on the ancestral line, but beyond that, children were expendable.

It would never have crossed the minds of many in Paul's world to offer expectations for husbands and fathers, much less slave owners. Their authority was absolute. They could do whatever they wanted to those beneath them. Society expected wives, children, and slaves to accept their positions and bow to whatever their superiors demanded. To that world, Paul issues a call to a new standard, a new way of life. He wipes away the distinctions between superior and inferior and challenges all followers of Jesus to "submit to one another." Within the Christian community, this is the universal standard!

It is also important to note that this passage has little to do with the roles of men and women, in general, in the church. Paul uses the relationship of husband and wife within a Christian marriage as an illustration of "submitting to one another." He pointedly says, "To your own husband." Nowhere does this imply that all men have authority over all women in the church or anywhere else. That is not the point. Of course, the principle of appropriate mutual submission to one another applies in congregational life.

Paul cites the fact that the husband is the "head" of the wife as the reason. He compares it to the role of Christ and the church, a relationship he will come back to in a moment. "Head" can imply many things. As with almost all words, however, definition must be determined by the context, not the dictionary. "Head" clearly carries a dimension of authority. Paul makes this clear in his discussion of Christ and the church elsewhere in Ephesians (1:22-23).

Submission and Responsibility

Perhaps it would be better to emphasize responsibility instead of authority. The husband has a special responsibility for his wife. As Paul will go on to say, a husband should sacrifice for his wife and even give himself for her. The wife needs to acknowledge and respect that. She must cooperate with him and not undermine his efforts. Hers is a responding love. Her "fear," like that of all believers toward the Lord, is grateful honor and respect. In a Christ-honoring marriage, "fear" should never be a terror-filled response to abuse and mistreatment. Another point of grammar—the participle or verb translated as "submit" is a middle voice. It is something the Christian wife voluntarily does. It can't be forced. A Christian husband can't demand it.

The theme remains—how Christians "submit to one another." This is the second illustration, the counterpart to the first. The fact that Paul includes this is perhaps the most noteworthy part. Few non-Christian writers in his day would have thought it proper to put any expectations on a "free male." They sat at the top of the social pecking order. The husband reigned as king of his castle. Period.

Christian husbands submit to their wives by loving them. Remember, all of the six case studies are an amplification of vs. 21—how Spirit-filled believers submit to one another. As in all the illustrations, this is about putting the other person first and serving their interests before our own. That is what submission is—placing ourselves in the subservient position. We acknowledge that the other person outranks us. In whatever role we are talking about, I am to consider myself a servant. I am to do the serving. I shouldn't expect to be served.

The fact that Paul uses the word "love" rather than submit doesn't lessen the demand at all. The common New Testament term for "love"—*agape*—described a sacrificial, giving, other-oriented affection. It didn't spring from emotion, status, or the hope that the "lover" would receive anything in return. This kind of love flowed from the character of the "lover," not from the merits of the one being loved.

Christ provides the perfect model for the Christian husband. Jesus loved and sacrificed for his bride. He did it not for his own benefit but for the blessing of the ones he loved. His goal was not to elevate his own position but to transform his church into the picture-perfect bride. This is a metaphor, of course. The husband-bride relationship comes as close as any human partnership can to mirroring the affection and good intentions the Lord has for his people. He wants the best for them. He wants them to shine. He would do anything for them. If you have ever watched the face of a groom on his wedding day as he first sees his bride start down the aisle, you know exactly the attitude that Paul is attempting to capture. That's how a Christian husband should always think of his wife.

This husband's love is Christ-like. It is also selfish in a good sort of way. The Christian spouse should love his partner as he loves himself. No one has difficulty caring for themselves, at least no one in his right mind. That's the assumption of the Golden Rule—"love your neighbor as yourself" (Leviticus 29:18). If it is true that we will naturally take care of ourselves, then a husband should just as naturally take care of his wife. When we marry, husband and wife take on a unique kind of relationship. The bride and groom merge their identities, priorities, and dreams.

Married love becomes self-love because the two have become one. When Adam first set his eyes on Eve, he recognized she was special. "It is like she was made for me," he said, "like she is part of me." The narrator in Genesis explains that this is the very reason a husband and wife turn from their pasts, embrace their new futures together, and form one new identity. The two become one (Gn 2:24).

Paul calls this a profound mystery. Agur, the wise man of Proverbs, observed much the same truth. Commenting on the great wonders of life, he says, *"There are three things that are too amazing for me, four that I do not understand...."* He lists three common examples. The fourth he intends as the most wonderful of all, *"the way of a man with a young woman"* (Prv 30:18-19). Few things in life are more powerful and transforming than when a man discovers true love for the woman of his dreams.

I witnessed this years ago in a striking way. Early in ministry, I worked with college students at what was primarily an engineering school. Consequently, the vast majority of the students were male, at least 80 percent. This created a problem for the guys who were interested in a dating relationship. Not so much for the girls! As the coeds were known to say, "The odds are good; but goods are odd." As with any environment where males outnumber females so disproportionately, a lot of things deteriorate fairly rapidly—attitudes, social skills, and sometimes hygiene. Guys without any girls to impress soon decide to quit trying. After a while, many of the male students stopped shaving, doing laundry as often, and, unfortunately, bathing. This wasn't universal, but it was definitely noticeable. But occasionally, I would witness a strange phenomenon. I would meet one of the guys on campus and he would be dressed in his finest shirt and tie, shaved and hair combed, and smelling like a perfume factory.

After a few such encounters, I quickly discovered that this new behavior was nearly always because of one of three reasons. First, he had a job interview. Or, he had worn the last of his regular duds and hadn't had a chance to do his laundry (or hadn't been home for his mom to do it!) and was left with nothing to wear but his Sunday-go-to-meeting clothes. Or finally, (Drum roll, please!) he had met a girl and finally had a date! The amazing sight of a young man and a young woman! Few things in life are more transforming. Indeed, a profound mystery!

But before Paul moves on from the Christian husband's responsibility toward their wives, his discussion takes a sharp turn. It is as if he were saying, "As wonderful and beautiful as the bond between a husband and wife is, I know something even more profound—that love relationship between Christ and his people." How could he possibly love us so much? How do you explain his sacrifice on the cross? How do you comprehend the amazing lengths to which our God goes to fashion our lives into the masterpiece he had planned from eternity? That's the ultimate measure of love.

Then Paul leaves a last word before moving on to the next case study of Spirit-filled submission. This may be a mystery. We might not be able to fully explain it. We will spend the rest of our lives working on it. *However!* Here's the bottom line—Husbands love your wives as yourself. Wives respect your husbands. Christian marriage is a two-way street. The words from John Peterson's wedding hymn say it best, "Each for the other; both for the Lord!"

All In the Family

Marriage is the foundation of any society. Family and children come next. Get these two wrong and few other social issues matter. Almost everything in a well-ordered and happy community, including the church, depends on these two. Children learn from their parents. Parents are the first teachers, and probably the ultimate teachers, of the lessons in life that matter most. Children learn from actual instructions, from discipline, and from their parents' model. That's how children learn manners, values, and proper relationships with other people. Pity the poor child who has everything life has to offer except what really matters.

The commandment to honor and obey one's parents forms the bridge commandment in the lessons handed down from Sinai (Ex 20). This child-parent principle rests between those relating to God and those relating to society at large. Paul calls this the first commandment with a promise. It's the only one of the Ten with an explicit blessing attached. "Long life" might be literal or figurative. Clearly, all things being equal, a child who learns the right lessons of life in a well-ordered family can look forward to a life long in quantity or quality, probably both.

For most ancient families, this next instruction would have been a bit surprising. As noted earlier, patriarchy reigned supreme in Greco-Roman society. Fathers were in charge. No one questioned their authority. A father often quite literally held the keys to the life and death of his children. Even brutality and abuse went unchallenged. But not in a Christian home. That's Paul's point. Christians must rise above the normal. They must set a different example.

Likely, Paul doesn't mention mothers in this directive because it wouldn't have been necessary. Patriarchy made the mentioning of mothers beside the point. Perhaps also, Paul recognizes the primary source of the problem. Mothers can become abusive. No one denies that. But on average, most mothers more naturally show love and nurture their children. Maybe those nine months before birth help generate that caring bond between mother and child. A father has to work a bit harder, or at least in a different way, to learn the skills needed for good parenting. Paul makes it clear that parenting requires involved dads. A Christian father, concerned about living a "Spirit-filled" life, can never abdicate his job and say, "I'm too busy. That's a mother's job." Parenting, at its best, requires two people: mom and dad.

The instruction makes an interesting emphasis. "*Do not exasperate your children.*" Other translations render the phrase, "*Do not provoke your children to anger.*" That keyword contains the idea of anger or wrath. The parallel passage in Colossians reads, "*Fathers, do not embitter your children, or they will become discouraged*" (3:21). Exasperated, angry, jealous, bitter, discouraged—whatever you call it, it is never good. Every child has experienced it. Every parent has witnessed it.

The positive alternative is a father who takes responsibility for "bringing up" his children. He trains them. This involves positive direction and teaching. Rewards and punishment often follow. Overly negative training can easily lead to the bitterness or exasperation spoken of earlier. The word for "instruction" used here is sometimes rendered "admonition." It most often refers to a warning or corrective instruction. Perhaps the most important phrase in the entire discussion is "of the Lord." Ultimately, lasting spiritual instruction is what counts.

Of Servants and Masters

Any discussion of slavery evokes strong emotions on the part of modern readers. Most of us find it next to impossible to separate this topic from our society's ongoing racial divide. Those of us who are honest with ourselves know that the Civil War nor the Civil Rights crusades that followed a hundred years later solved the problem. Despite a lot of unpleasant history, we need to rid ourselves of as much of this baggage as we can as we approach Paul's last two case studies.

Slavery is always bad for the slave and often for the master. We dare not sugar-coat any form of human bondage. But ancient slavery differed from its modern counterpart in one very important way. Ancient slavery most often resulted from conquest. Two nations went to war. The winner enslaved the loser. As a result, slaves might include the best and the brightest of the defeated nation, the formerly rich, the highly educated, and the skilled craftsmen. The poor and illiterate might remain behind to do the heavy lifting in rebuilding the conquered land. These lower-level slaves would work the fields and mines, sending the wealth back to the victor. The higher-valued slaves would become teachers, translators, and artisans once they were brought back to the victorious nation.

Slavery was a fact of life in ancient Rome. Many estimate that slaves made up as much as twenty to thirty percent of the empire's population. The slaves worked in industrial and government projects, private homes as tutors, and servants. As always, the life of a slave was dictated by the character of the owner. If a slave had a kind owner, life might be tolerable. A cruel and depraved master, on the other hand, could make a slave's existence a living hell. A fair number of slaves gained freedom either by the goodwill of an owner or by amassing enough money to purchase their own liberty.

In many ancient civilizations, a form of slavery resulted from simple economics. Without the equivalent of bankruptcy, a person who found himself over his head in debt had few good choices. Often, he could settle the debt by selling himself into slavery for a prescribed number of years. In some cases, he might sell one of his children. Once the terms of the debt were satisfied, the slave might be freed. Of course, it was always better to never have to face such a choice.

The New Testament never advocated the abolition of slavery for one very obvious reason. That was not an option. The empire was not a democracy. Christians couldn't vote. Any threat to the status quo coming from criticizing slavery would be met with a certain and violent response from the powers that be. Instead, Paul and other believers advocated for an insurgency that would quietly undermine the institution of slavery from within. Paul did this in a number of ways.

First, he used the vocabulary. He referred to himself as a slave of Christ (Romans 1:1; 2 Cor 4:5; Phil 1:1). He even insisted that Christ took the form of a slave when he emptied himself and was made in the likeness of man (Phil 2:7). He gave slavery a new meaning. Secondly, he declared that in Christ, there was no longer slave or free (Gal 3:28). In the fellowship of the church, slaves and masters could worship together as equal servants of the one Lord.

Paul never suggested for a minute that slavery was a good thing. Quite the opposite! But he told any slave who became a Christian to concentrate on being the best Christian slave they could be (Ti 2:9-10). Freedom was not the ultimate goal. The main thing was to represent Christ in everything they did. But if they ever had the opportunity to be free, they should take it (1 Cor 7:21-24).

So how does a Christian slave demonstrate a Spirit-filled life in his relationship with a master? He should serve his master as if serving Christ. The slave's service should come from the heart. No longer is it enough to go through the motions. Maybe, a fresh attitude on the slave's part would improve the master's response. Maybe it wouldn't. Either way, the Christian slave's most important reward would come from his Lord and Savior. The Lord rewards faithfulness wherever it is found. The Christian, regardless of his status, should look for opportunities to bless and serve others, even a slave master!

Modern employment and ancient slavery have little in common. We shouldn't pretend that they do. However, Paul's counsel to slaves includes some important lessons for us. Our paycheck shouldn't determine how we do our job. We don't "quietly quit," putting in the hours but not the effort. We don't behave one way when the boss is looking and another when he isn't. Ultimately, we work for the Lord whether on the clock or off.

Masters Have a Master

Once a slave owner became a Christian, his world changed. His faith transformed that and every other relationship in his life—his marriage, his family, and the way he treated his slaves. That was a radical idea in that culture. But Paul doesn't back down from making such a demand. The master has a master. His ownership should reflect that fact. An owner could always set his slaves free. Sometimes, that might cause more problems than it solved. But regardless, threats, abuse, and violence of every sort must go. The owner must learn to treat his slaves the way he wanted to be treated. The Golden Rule allowed no exceptions.

If I believe God is at work, weaving a masterpiece according to his eternal purpose, then I must trust him to do his work and finish what he starts. I may not always see what he is doing. What God is doing may not always make sense to me at any given point. But if I am convinced that he is at work, that's enough.

Now, we are ready to hear Paul's last words. How does he say all that he has said and draw it to a close? Does he end with a bang or a whimper? Last words are hard.

✝

Chapter Thirteen: Battle Ready

Finally, be strong in the Lord and in his mighty power. Put on the full armor of God, so that you can take your stand against the devil's schemes. For our struggle is not against flesh and blood, but against the rulers, against the authorities, against the powers of this dark world and against the spiritual forces of evil in the heavenly realms. Therefore put on the full armor of God, so that when the day of evil comes, you may be able to stand your ground, and after you have done everything, to stand. Stand firm then, with the belt of truth buckled around your waist, with the breastplate of righteousness in place, and with your feet fitted with the readiness that comes from the gospel of peace. In addition to all this, take up the shield of faith, with which you can extinguish all the flaming arrows of the evil one. Take the helmet of salvation and the sword of the Spirit, which is the word of God.

And pray in the Spirit on all occasions with all kinds of prayers and requests. With this in mind, be alert and always keep on praying for all the Lord's people. Pray also for me, that whenever I speak, words may be given me so that I will fearlessly make known the mystery of the gospel, for which I am an ambassador in chains. Pray that I may declare it fearlessly, as I should.

*Tychicus, the dear brother and faithful servant in the
Lord, will tell you everything, so that you also may
know how I am and what I am doing. I am sending
him to you for this very purpose, that you may know
how we are, and that he may encourage you.*
*Peace to the brothers and sisters, [a] and love with faith
from God the Father and the Lord Jesus Christ. Grace
to all who love our Lord Jesus Christ with an undying
love.*

Ephesians 6:10-24

The last words matter. I can imagine Paul pausing as he finishes
the lines we've been considering. He stops and ponders what to
say next. He knows he needs to draw the letter to a close. But how?
He wants to leave them with something important. He wants to put
an exclamation point on everything that he has already said. Maybe
he decides to sleep on it and finish the letter the next morning.
Perhaps he would talk about it with Tychicus or other of his friends
allowed to visit him. He would certainly pray over his letter before
he finished.

Paul probably went over the letter again, perhaps even reading it
through word for word. Early in the letter, he had reminded them
what God had been doing to bring them to where they were. God
had a plan and a purpose, Paul had said. Their Lord was thinking
of them even before they had ever given any thought to him. All
that God had done in Christ was for them. He was at work even
though they might not always be able to see it. If they could see the
hand of God at work, they would be so amazed! Paul had told them,
*"I pray that the eyes of your heart may be enlightened in order that
you may know the hope to which he has called you, the riches of
his glorious inheritance in his holy people"* (1:18).

Paul had written about the radical transformation God had brought about in their individual lives. He had brought them from death to life. It was all of grace. They couldn't take any credit for what he had done. And he wasn't finished. God was still at work, fashioning a masterpiece out of each of their lives. *"For we are God's handiwork, created in Christ Jesus to do good works, which God prepared in advance for us to do"* (2:10).

The Exclamation Point at the End

Paul turns to military jargon to close his letter. Perhaps he does so for the contrast. This is unlike anything else he had written thus far. Maybe he decides to add some shock value to his closing to get their attention. On the other hand, the time spent thinking about how to end the letter might have given him a fresh dose of reality. He was a prisoner of the empire. A soldier stood guard at his door night and day. As he thought about his personal fate and the future facing his friends in far-off Ephesus, he was forced to face the facts. This was not a game. This was war!

It is unlikely that Paul had ever served in the army, but he had undoubtedly been around quite a few soldiers. He had been in more than a few jails and prisons in his life, always guarded by current or former soldiers. No doubt, he engaged in a few late-night conversations with his guards. It was only fair that he listened to their story in exchange for an opportunity to tell his. Of course, his story was always more about Jesus and less about himself. At any rate, he probably had a lot of secondhand information about military life.

What Every Soldier Knows

Paul knew that among the cardinal rules of Roman military life were three essentials. First, a soldier must keep the mission front and center. Everything else paled in importance. Hadn't he been telling the Ephesians this from the beginning of his letter? God had a purpose. Their job was to follow that plan and fulfill it in their church and their lives. Second, unit cohesion matters. If a company of soldiers didn't stand together, they would certainly fall together. That had been his theme throughout the letter. Unity mattered. It didn't just make life more pleasant. In the heat of battle, unity meant survival. Finally, every warrior needs to know the enemy. Paul had hinted at this a bit in what he had written, but now he wants to make sure there is no misunderstanding. He wants his readers to know who the enemy is and who it isn't.

Paul's final words are organized around a series of imperatives/commands. All are battle orders. Be strong (Vs. 10). Put on the full armor (Vs. 11 and 13). Stand firm (Vs. 14). Take (Vs. 17). Each command links to one central reason stated in verse 12—"For our battle is not against flesh and blood."

Knowing Our Real Enemy

In the fog of war, it is easy to lose sight of the real enemy. Paul terms the enemy—"the schemes of the devil," "rulers, powers, the world forces of darkness, the spiritual forces of wickedness in the heavenly places." He knew that reality consisted of more than meets the eye. Real spiritual forces were at work behind the scenes in ways that we little understand. Earlier, he had insisted that before

Christ made us alive, we all had lived under the direction of the "prince of the power of the air" (2:2). We may not see the hand of the devil at work, but his fingerprints are everywhere.

We can make two big mistakes when speaking of the devil. We can ignore him and pretend he doesn't exist. Our disbelief doesn't eliminate the problem. On the other hand, we can be preoccupied with all things satanic. We think we can't fight a spiritual battle until we know everything there is to be known about Satan. We can fall victim to "paralysis of analysis." On the other hand, we can think and talk about him so much that we begin to imagine him everywhere. We can get to the point where we know him better than we know our Lord. That's never good!

When we obsess about the devil, we overestimate him. We imagine him to be more powerful than he really is. We can quickly give up, thinking that since we are bound to lose anyway, why try? Imagined familiarity can lead to underestimation as well. Tragically, some of us conclude that once we are sufficiently schooled in the ways of Satan, we are ready to handle him on our own. That's the last thing we should conclude. Or worse yet, we mistake fellow victims for the enemy and quickly take up arms against the walking wounded.

The battle is not political, though politics can be the scene of spiritual conflict like every other arena of human activity. Sadly, recent history has witnessed increased conflict and division over politics, even in the church. As hard as it is for some to believe, if you are a Democrat, your enemy is not the Republicans, and vice versa. The problem with thinking that the root problem or the ultimate solution is politics is that we put too much hope and energy into that battle. We are deceived into believing that if we could just pass the right laws, or put the right judges on the Supreme Court, or elect a different president, or you name the political change, then everything would be perfect again, just like "the good old days." The battle is not against "flesh and blood!"

The battle is not economic. Many think it is. Clearly, wages and prices, the corn market, the stock market, and interest rates all matter. Of course, your checkbook and credit card balances affect everything you do. But the world's biggest problems would not be solved if suddenly poverty were eliminated. But that is not an excuse for a stingy, self-serving attitude. Of course, we ought to work toward a more just and honest society. While the love of money may be the root of many problems, possessing it solves few of our ultimate issues.

If the battle is not against "flesh and blood," then we are not at war with other religious groups. Too many real wars have been fought in the name of religion. On top of that, countless arguments have been waged and tears shed in the bloodless conflicts between denominations—all in the name of Christ. How tragic! Our enemy is not the church down the street with a different name or believers who disagree with us over things we hold dear. When we begin to think that our real enemies are our neighbors with different traditions, we shut the door on ever sharing the good news of Jesus with them. As a result, we often turn our backs on the real adversary.

Your Neighbor Is Not Your Enemy

Maybe, most important of all, we are not in a battle with one another. According to the story, famous British general Lord Nelson was readying his men for an important battle. He overheard two of his officers in a heated argument. He called them to his tent and said, "Gentlemen, give me your hands." The two captains put their hands in the commander's hands. He squeezed them with a tight vice-like grip, looked them in the eye, and said, "Men, remember the ENEMY is OUT THERE!"

In his call to arms, Paul issues four commands. The first, "be strong in the Lord and in his mighty power" (6:10). This is the key. Since the battle is spiritual, we are not going to win it on our own. This has been Paul's message throughout the letter—God's got this! Knowing that is the first command. Self-reliance and self-sufficiency spell certain defeat.

Don't Take a Knife to a Gunfight

The enemy is spiritual, not flesh and blood. He works his schemes and multiplies his lies behind the scenes, largely unseen. Since the battlefield is spiritual, so should be the weapons. This may be Paul's main point. "Don't take a knife to a gunfight," they say in the movies. It is just as foolish to go to battle with the spiritual forces of evil with the wrong weapons. Paul is now ready to explain how to take up arms for this spiritual battle.

The second command in Paul's last words is "to put on the full armor of God." The weapons come from God's armory, not ours. No instruments of human warfare will do. The battle is the Lord's. Also, the conflict requires the "full armor of God." We can't afford to pick and choose what we think we need. Our commander insists that everything on the list is essential.

A fully equipped soldier will be ready for whatever comes. He can withstand the worst the enemy can throw his way. It is not enough to be prepared for a little skirmish. We must be prepared for an all-out war. We want to still be standing no matter how long the conflict or dangerous the threat.

Also, note that the conflict appears to be defensive. The list contains no offensive weapons—no bow and arrows, no javelins, no catapults or long-distance arms of any sort. Even the two-edged sword was designed for hand-to-hand combat. The battle will be up close and personal. The weapons listed are for holding ground already taken. The battle is the Lord's. He has already taken the invasion to the enemy. His victory on the cross and the resurrection have already captured the enemy's stronghold and set the captives free. It is not up to us to conquer anyone or anything. We hold the ground he has taken. God's got this!

So what spiritual weapons does Paul insist we need for our battle? He lists six. Each might have been part of an ordinary Roman soldier's battle dress. Paul could have been describing what he saw as he studied the men who guarded him day in and day out. On the other hand, most of the images Paul uses come straight out of the Hebrew Scriptures. Isaiah described the belt of righteousness and the sash of faithfulness worn by the coming

Messiah (11:5). The prophet later announced that the Lord himself would do battle against wickedness. *"He put on righteousness as his breastplate, and the helmet of salvation on his head; he put on the garments of vengeance and wrapped himself in zeal as in a cloak"* (59:17).

Outfitted from the Armory of God

Let's take a closer look at the six pieces of spiritual armor we need for our conflict "against the spiritual forces of evil in the heavenly realms." Paul possibly lists the items in the order a soldier might dress for battle. First, he dons the belt of truth. The literal belt, in this case, might have been the leather strap that held the warrior's garments tight and out of the way. Any other tools and weapons would hang from this belt. Without it, little else mattered.

Paul refers to it as the belt of *truth*. In the spiritual battle, everything stands or falls on the validity of the gospel. We were saved when we heard the word of truth (Eph 1:13). We live out our faith based on the truth we have been taught about Jesus (Eph 4:21). In our new life in Christ, we were "created to be like God in true righteousness and holiness" (Eph 5:24). Consequently, the life we live must shine bright with "goodness and righteousness and truth" (Eph 5:9). First things first! We stand on the truth of Christ and endeavor to live that truth. Everything else hangs on this.

Next comes the breastplate of *righteousness* or right standing before the judgment of God. Any righteousness that we possess comes from Christ. Like Paul, we have learned that we have no claim to it on our own (Phil 3:9). Yet our goal and aim in life is "to pursue righteousness" (1 Tm 6:11). We want to be pleasing in our Lord's sight more than anything else. A breastplate consisted of a plate of metal or, later, chain mail strapped to the soldier's body. Ideally, the breastplate protected his vital organs from injury. In our spiritual conflict, righteousness, Christ's and ours that comes from faith in him alone, guards our heart and everything else that is vital to our faith. If we forsake righteousness and stand naked and unprotected before the assault on our souls, all will be lost.

Every army depends on good shoes. A soldier with sore feet or boots without a firm footing seldom wins the day. That's where Paul turns next. Standing firm requires having our feet "fitted with the readiness that comes from the gospel of peace" (6:15). A typical Roman soldier wore leather sandals or boots with studs driven through the soles. These gripped the ground so that his feet would not slip out from under him in the heat of battle. The Christian warrior stands on the "gospel of peace," the good news of God found in Christ. Our firm foundation rests in what Christ has done. When we are planted in Him, we can "*always be prepared to give an answer to everyone who asks you to give the reason for the hope that you have*" (1 Pt 3:15).

The shield of *faith* comes next. For the Roman legions, this shield was a large wooden oval, about the size of a door, covered in leather and drenched in water before the battle. When placed together, the shields of a platoon of soldiers would form a wall or, if held overhead, a roof. The wet leather protected the soldier from incoming arrows, sometimes ablaze with tar or oil. That's what faith does for the Christian soldier, Paul insists. It deflects the worst the enemy can throw our way. We face the enemy confidently, knowing that God is in control. We trust his protection. Our enemy will attack. No question about that. But when he does, God's got this!

Two more items from God's armory must be taken up before we engage the enemy. We must put on *"the helmet of salvation."* Helmets were hot and cumbersome. A soldier might be tempted to set it aside. But any hesitation to wear it into battle could be fatal. The helmet protected the head. Every Christian warrior needs to know where he stands with his Savior before he meets the enemy. Our confidence rests in knowing *"there is now no condemnation for those in Christ"* (Romans 8:1). With Paul, we can affirm that *"I know whom I have believed, and am convinced that he is able to guard what I have entrusted to him until that day"* (2 Tm 1:12). Second thoughts about our future or God's faithfulness leave us vulnerable to Satan's assault.

One last piece fills out the equipment list—*"the sword of the Spirit."* Literally, this referred to the small, double-edged sword a soldier carried for hand-to-hand conflict. Ultimately, it might be his last defense. Paul calls this "the word of God." But the term used here refers to a spoken word, not necessarily the written word. Having a Bible is one thing. Knowing it well enough to recall and speak its message is another. Perhaps this is what Revelation means when it declares that the saints triumphed over Satan "by the blood of the Lamb and by the word of their testimony" (12:11). No believer dares go into battle unarmed.

Lest we forget that this is a spiritual battle we face, Paul concludes with one more essential ingredient that can easily be passed over. He mentions prayer last, not because it is secondary to the other items. In fact, it undergirds all that has gone before. For the

Christian, prayer needs to become our first impulse and not our last option once we have tried everything else.

Praying "*in the Spirit*" likely describes another dimension of living "under the influence" that Paul had described earlier. We pray, knowing that the Spirit of God is working in and around us. We are not acting alone—especially when we pray. He intercedes for us when words escape us (Rm 8:26-27). Note the "alls" in Paul's call to prayer—*on all occasions with all kinds of prayer and requests...for all the Lord's people.* No request is too small or too big. No situation is too dire or too simple for our attention or God's. No brother or sister is beyond the need of another's prayer. Our God wants us to turn to him in prayer. Any reluctance exists on our part, not his.

When we promise to pray for one another, we have each other's back. Nothing reassures a soldier on the frontlines more than knowing he's not alone. No matter what happens, his fellow soldiers will be right there at his side. That's why Paul doesn't leave the topic of prayer without asking his friends to pray for him. He doesn't ask them to pray for his release from prison, though I am sure that was on their minds and his. He asks for opportunities to speak for Christ. He wants them to pray for his courage and boldness. The last thing he wants is to falter in a moment of crisis.

* * *

Paul concludes with a personal note. This is a letter, after all. But a letter seldom replaces real face-to-face interaction. Tychicus would personally carry this letter to the Ephesian church and likely others, along with one for the Colossians (Col 4:7-8). We know little about this Christian brother other than he was a companion and co-laborer with the apostle (Acts 20:4; 2 Tm 4:12; Ti 3:12). Paul commends him as a faithful servant of the Lord.

Paul knew what we often forget. Our faith was never meant to be lived alone. We simply can't do it on our own. We need God's help, but a big part of what he wishes to do in our lives is through the body of Christ, our brothers and sisters. A solo Christian is a vulnerable Christian and often an ineffective one. Together, we are strong. Alone, we are weak.

Paul concludes most of his letters with a benediction, a parting prayer of blessing. He prays peace and love for them. But he can't finish without pointing to the grand theme with which he had begun his letter—grace. Grace forms the bookends that frame all that he has had to say. We are redeemed by the riches of his grace (1:7). We have been saved by his grace (2:8-9). We live for the praise of his grace (1:6). We serve one another out of the gifts of his grace (4:7). We speak words of grace as we share life together (4:29). All that we are and all that we have in Christ come from one source—God's grace.

* * *

The Masterpiece the Master Weaves

We may live on the underside of the tapestry. From our vantage point, it can be hard to see what the Maker has in mind. But our side is not the only side. God is at work. He knows what we don't.

He sees what we can't. Even when life seems totally out of control, it isn't.

Paul's beautiful letter known to us as Ephesians explains how God is at work weaving a masterpiece out of the chaos of life (Eph 2:10). He is not finished. He has much more to do. Masterpieces are fashioned at the intersection of grace, servanthood, and the sovereignty of God.

Endnotes

[1] C.S. Lewis, "They Asked for a Paper" in *Is Theology Poetry?* (London: Geoffrey Bliss, 1962). 165.

[2] C.S. Lewis, *The Problem of Pain* (San Francisco: HarperSanFran, 1940; reprint 2001), 91.

[3] Soren Kierkegaard, *Purity of the Heart Is to Will One Thing* (New York: Start Publishing LLC, 2012), 1940-1962, Kindle.

About the Author

Will Thomas (DMin, Northern Seminary) is an adopted son of the Lone Star State. He grew up on a pig farm and worked his way through college as a construction worker. Will even spent time on the dark side as a dreaded telemarketer and a persistent Aflac agent. On the brighter side, he has served as a campus minister, pastor, church planter, college professor, and newspaper columnist. Will is the author of seven books and hundreds of magazine articles in dozens of publications, including Christianity Today, Eternity, His, Christian Standard, The Disciple, Preaching, Worldwide Challenge, Restoration Herald, and many others. In addition, his work has appeared in the widely read Chicken Soup for the Soul series. What you might not know, Will plays a six-eight power forward for the Dallas Mavericks—in his dreams.